ALSO BY LISA LILLIEN

● ●

Hungry Girl:
Recipes and Survival Strategies for
Guilt-Free Eating in the Real World

Hungry Girl 200 Under 200:
200 Recipes Under 200 Calories

Hungry Girl 1-2-3:
The Easiest, Most Delicious,
Guilt-Free Recipes on the Planet

Hungry Girl Happy Hour:
75 Recipes for Amazingly Fantastic
Guilt-Free Cocktails & Party Foods

Hungry Girl 300 Under 300:
300 Breakfast, Lunch & Dinner
Dishes Under 300 Calories

Hungry Girl Chew the Right Thing:
Supreme Makeovers for 50 Foods You Crave
(recipe cards)

Hungry Girl:
The Official Survival Guides:
Tips & Tricks for Guilt-Free Eating
(audio book)

Supermarket SURVIVAL

AISLE BY AISLE, HG-STYLE!

* **Lisa Lillien** *

St. Martin's Griffin
New York

HUNGRY GIRL SUPERMARKET SURVIVAL: AISLE BY AISLE, HG-STYLE! Copyright © 2011 by Hungry Girl, Inc. All rights reserved. Printed in the United States of America. For information, address St. Martin's Press, 175 Fifth Avenue, New York, N.Y. 10010.

www.stmartins.com

Cover design and book design by Elizabeth Hodson

Illustrations by Jack Pullan

ISBN 978-0-312-67673-5

First Edition: October 2011

10 9 8 7 6 5 4 3 2 1

THIS BOOK IS
DEDICATED TO
CONFUSED
SUPERMARKET
SHOPPERS
EVERYWHERE.

CONTENTS

ACKNOWLEDGMENTS

I'd like to thank the HG staffers, who worked insanely hard on this incredibly helpful shopping guide . . .

Jamie Goldberg
Dana DeRuyck
Samantha Oliver
Lynn Bettencourt
Callie Pegadiotes
Lisa Friedman
Michelle Ferrand
Melissa Klotz
Amanda Pisani

and the best book designer of all time . . .
Elizabeth Hodson

The following enjoyable people also deserve credit . . .

In alphabetical order:
Jeff Becker, Jen Enderlin, Tom Fineman, John Karle, Alison Kreuch, Neeti Madan, John Murphy, Jack Pullan, Matthew Shear, Bill Stankey, Anne Marie Tallberg, and John Vaccaro.

And special thanks to . . .
My amazing husband, Daniel Schneider; my wonderful parents, Florence & Maurice Lillien; Meri Lillien; Jay Lillien; and the entire Lillien & Schneider families.

WELCOME TO HUNGRY GIRL SUPERMARKET ☑ SURVIVAL!

• •

This is your guide to navigating the supermarket aisles. Inside this book you'll find all the tips, tricks, product finds, charts, calorie counts, and shockers you'll ever need for guilt-free eating in the real world!

GUILT-FREE EATING IN THE REAL WORLD?

Time to face facts: America eats processed food. These foods tempt us all day, every day. And while a strict diet comprised only of "clean foods" works well for certain people, it's unrealistic to expect the masses to flip a switch and only shop the perimeter of the market. Some of the foods in this book are 100 percent natural; some are not. There's a huge emphasis on easy and delicious ways to fill your diet with fruit, veggies, lean protein, low-fat dairy, and whole grains. There are also many products and recommendations to help fulfill real-world cravings for fattening things like fried food, pizza, cookies, and chips without taking in a crazy amount of calories and fat. In other words, these can help you to maintain a healthy weight without feeling deprived. Hungry Girl provides a happy medium—a bridge between the average junk-food diet and the idealistic way of eating perfectly healthy at all times. It's a realistic approach to better-for-you eating that people can actually live with and feel good about.

THE 411 ON HUNGRY GIRL . . .

Hungry Girl is a free daily email subscription service about guilt-free eating. The emails (which are read by over a million people a day) feature news, food finds, recipes, and real-world survival strategies. Hungry Girl was started by me, Lisa Lillien. I'm not a doctor or nutrition professional; I'm just hungry! Back in 2004, I decided I wanted to share my love and knowledge of guilt-free eating with the world, so Hungry Girl was born. To sign up for the daily emails or to see what you've missed since the beginning, go to **Hungry-Girl.com**.

Enjoy this book and all of your future trips to the supermarket . . . Happy chewing!

DAIRY

~ CHEESE ~

* NEED-TO-KNOW LINGO *
CHEESE EDITION

Reduced-fat, **2% milk**, and **33% less fat** all indicate the same thing—cheese with *at least* 25% less fat than standard cheese.

Low-fat, on the other hand, is pretty specific—3 grams of fat or less per serving!

Fat-Free and Reduced-Fat Shredded Cheese

The fat-free kind is a major calorie bargain, but flavor options are limited and it doesn't melt quite as well as the reduced-fat cheeses. Opt for fat-free shreds (cheddar is a supermarket staple) when you're topping an already decadent dish or when meltability isn't a concern. Choose reduced-fat cheese when your snack or meal calls for more richness—you'll find the reduced-fat version a lot more flavorful.

HG Standout: Any brand of 2% milk **Mexican-blend cheese.** The mix of mild and zesty cheeses is fantastic for easily infusing cheesy Mexican flavor into dishes.

HG Tip: Before grabbing that part-skim mozzarella, consider light string cheese. While the shreds are good for multi-serve recipes that call for a sizable measured amount, light string cheese offers the same great flavor and meltability—and it's portion-controlled. Check out **page 8** in this section for more info on this.

Fat-Free and Reduced-Fat Slices

Unlike no-fat *shreds*, fat-free *slices* melt very well, making them perfect for burgers and open-faced sandwich melts. They're also great for when you want to keep the fat count down in dishes that include some decadent ingredients. The reduced-fat slices are better for snacking on straight. And they do offer up a better taste when it comes to Swiss cheese, so those can be worth the splurge for Reubens and other sandwiches that call for Swiss.

HG Tip: If you're easily lured in by open packs of deli slices, consider the individually wrapped singles instead.

Fat-Free and Reduced-Fat Block-Style Cheese

Fat-free cheese you shred yourself typically melts much better than the pre-shredded kind. It's also fantastic for making stovetop cheese sauces with a little light soymilk. The reduced-fat blocks are great for snacking and often cheaper than pre-wrapped individual snacks—but if you can't be trusted to keep portions in check, the savings likely aren't worth it.

HG Standout: Lifetime makes an amazing assortment of fat-free block-style cheese, including flavors you typically can't find without fat, like Monterey Jack.

→ The Fat & Calorie 411 ←
for Shreds, Slices, Etc.

Read labels and seek out cheeses with the following stats . . .

Fat-Free Cheese
1 slice = 25 to 30 calories
1 ounce (¼ cup) shreds = 45 calories
1 ounce (a 1-inch cube) block cheese = 45 calories

Reduced-Fat Cheese
1 slice = 40 to 60 calories and 2.5 to 4.5 grams of fat
1 ounce (¼ cup) shreds = 60 to 80 calories and 5 to 6 grams of fat
1 ounce (a 1-inch cube) block cheese = 60 to 80 calories and
    5 to 6 grams of fat

Reduced-Fat Cheese Snacks

Portion-controlled cheeses are ideal for protein-packed snacking on the go, but stick with ones that have 100 calories or less. Look for firm types, like cheddar cubes and jalapeño jack sticks, and semi-soft stuff too, like this next Hungry Girl favorite . . .

 **HG All-Star!**

Mini Babybel Light. These are the wax-encased cheese rounds that come packed in white nets. Each one has 50 calories and 3 grams of fat, and their protective red wax makes them perfect for tossing into your purse, backpack, or toting device of choice. The regular (not Light) varieties are delicious too; just know that those have 60 to 80 calories and 5 to 6 grams of fat each.

Light String Cheese

The word "light" should lead you right to the versions with 50 to 60 calories and about 2.5 grams of fat each. Typically part-skim mozzarella, these pull-apart treats are amazing—not only as snacks, but in recipes too. They melt terrifically once torn into pieces, laid over your favorite foods, and baked, toasted, or broiled.

Best Tip Ever: String Cheese in a Blender!

Break a stick of the light stuff into thirds, and toss into a mini food processor or blender. Pulse to a shredded/grated consistency. The result is an ideal amount of fluffy cheese with superior meltability for making personal pizzas, Italian-style scrambles, English-muffin melts, and chicken Parmesan. Mmmmm!

Fat-Free and Reduced-Fat Crumbled Feta Cheese

These little flavor-packed morsels go a long way. Great for salads and Greek-inspired recipes. A ¼-cup serving of the fat-free crumbles has just about 35 calories. The reduced-fat kind typically contains 60 to 70 calories and 4 grams of fat per ¼ cup.

HG FYI:

Look for seasoned types, like basil and garlic. Or just buy plain and season it yourself.

⭐ HG All-Star!
The Laughing Cow Light Cheese Wedges

With 35 calories and 1.5 to 2 grams of fat each, these foil-wrapped wedges are in a category all their own. They're spreadable, meltable, super-creamy, and deliciously mild. They're packed in 8-wedge wheels emblazoned with a giddy red cow. The Creamy Swiss is classic, but there are several other flavors . . . ALL worth trying! There are similar products out there, but the kinds by The Laughing Cow are truly the best.

HG's TOP ATE Uses for
The Laughing Cow Light Cheese Wedges

1. Four words: omelettes, scrambles, egg mugs!
   (See Egg-Mug/Egg-Scramble Essentials, page 205.)
2. As a cream cheese swap!
3. In gooey-good quesadillas made with high-fiber tortillas.
4. Mixed with fat-free sour cream and reduced-fat Parmesan-style grated topping for a guilt-free Alfredo sauce.
5. Stuffed inside homemade burger patties made from lean turkey or extra-lean beef.
6. Spread on apple slices and paired with other fruits.
7. Mixed with salsa or fat-free refried beans to make a creamy queso dip!
8. In cheese-infused scoopable salads and spreads made with tuna, salmon, or crab. Yum!

Fat-Free Cream Cheese

Seek out the round tubs as opposed to the rectangular blocks. Why? Because this stuff is best when melted and mixed with other things, and the tub product is softer and easier to work with. When you're craving a classic schmear, The Laughing Cow Light cheese wedges really are an ideal swap. But FFCC has its place in your shopping cart—it's a valuable component when making extra-creamy fillings, sauces, desserts, and more. Each 2-tablespoon serving has about 30 calories.

HG FYI:
There's no such thing as "low-fat" cream cheese. The reduced-fat/light kind packs 70 calories and 5 to 6 grams of fat per 2-tablespoon serving. That's more than twice the calories of fat-free cream cheese, and a little steep for a simple spread.

Fat-Free, Low-Fat, and Light Ricotta Cheese

This creamy, mildly flavored stuff is wildly underrated. Use it in dessert recipes in place of fattening mascarpone—just add a little vanilla extract, no-calorie sweetener, and some room-temp fat-free cream cheese. Mix it with savory spices and use as a creamy filling for stuffed mushrooms or as an ingredient in casseroles.

Devilishly Deceptive: Part-Skim. Skip It!

Fat-free ricotta can be a bit elusive, but its nutritionals are seriously impressive—¼ cup contains about 45 calories. The low-fat and light kinds are common and completely reasonable, with an average of 60 calories and just 2.5 grams of fat per ¼ cup. Just know that part-skim is not the same; that has 70 to 90 calories and 4.5 to 6 grams of fat. Big difference!

Fat-Free and Low-Fat Cottage Cheese

With 80 to 100 calories and impressive protein stats (about 13 grams) per ½-cup serving, this creamy, scoopable stuff is an ideal staple for snacking. Add flavor and sweetness with sweet spices and extracts (try cinnamon and vanilla), fruit (fresh, juice-packed and drained, or thawed from frozen), and a little sweetener. Great for no-cook breakfasts and parfaits too. In addition to the tubs, look for single-serving containers—perfect for snacks on the go and as mini-fridge staples.

Fun Find: Fruit on the Side!

Look for individual containers of the low-fat stuff with sidecars of sweet and fruity add-ins, like Knudsen/Breakstone's Cottage Doubles. Sure there are pre-mixed fruit-infused cottage cheese cups, but these are just a little more fun (and better for control freaks) . . .

Cheese Alternatives:
Almond Cheese and Soy Cheese

Despite being made with nuts or beans, these can be fantastically low in fat and completely delicious. But they require a few heads-ups . . .

1. **Not all alterna-cheeses are created equal.** Read the nutritional panels to ensure they meet your guilt-free standards. Look for those similar in stats to reduced-fat cheese—some of our favorites (the standouts listed below) are even lower!

2. **These aren't always dairy-free.** If you're lactose-intolerant or sensitive to dairy, read through those ingredient lists. Do it before you chew it . . .

3. **They may be hard to find.** If you don't see them near the regular cheese, look for them with the refrigerated tofu, soy-based products, specialty foods, or gourmet cheeses.

> **HG Standouts:** Lisanatti Foods The Original Almond Cheese Alternative and Galaxy Nutritional Foods Veggie Shreds, Slices, and Blocks.

Don't Forget . . .

 to swing by the pasta aisle for reduced-fat Parmesan-style grated topping. With just 30 calories per tablespoon, this product adds major flavor to all sorts of recipes. Use it as a topping or stir it into soups, sauces, and more.

☑ **to stock up on frozen veggies in low-fat cheese sauce.** For a quick and easy side dish with built-in cheesy goodness or a saucy start to veggie-loaded recipes! You can find these in single-serving trays and multi-serving bags and boxes. Green Giant's Just for One options are some of the best in the biz.

~ YOGURT ~

Fat-Free Fruity and Desserty Yogurt

Look for single-serving containers (usually 6 ounces) with 110 calories or less. These are fantastic snack staples to keep in the fridge. They also make ideal ingredients for super-easy recipes like smoothies and parfaits. Look for flavors inspired by whichever fattening desserts you crave, like banana cream pie, apple turnovers, or blueberry cobbler. And don't discount classic vanilla. YUM!

HG Heads-Up
Not all fat-free yogurt is low in calories—some brands have as many as 160 calories per 6-ounce serving. So read those labels!

HG Standout: Yoplait Light. It's our hands-down, go-to yogurt line. Amazing flavor options, rich and creamy texture, and all-around delicious. **Yoplait Fiber One** ROCKS too!

Fat-Free Plain Yogurt

It may seem boring, but this stuff is fantastic in so many ways. Add some seasoning and use it as marinade for lean meats; it'll make your protein of choice insanely tender and delicious. It's also good in tangy cream sauces, sweet salad dressings, and anywhere else you want to add creamy texture and a touch of tartness without a specific flavor attached. For a sweet snack, mix in things like fruit and sweetener. Look for yogurt with 110 calories or less per 6-ounce serving. If you use it often, go for the larger tubs, with a 1-cup (8-ounce) serving size—then your calorie count should be about 130.

HG SHOCKER!

Think yogurt can't be too bad in the stats department? Guess again. A cup of full-fat yogurt can have around **200 calories** and **8 grams of fat** . . . READ THOSE LABELS!

Fat-Free and Low-Fat Plain Greek Yogurt

Greek yogurt undergoes a straining process that results in a SUPER-THICK consistency. Compared to regular fat-free yogurt, it has more protein (about 20 grams per cup, nearly twice as much as regular), fewer carbs, less sodium, and less sugar—although standard yogurt does have more calcium. There's room for both in our fridge! What else makes it special? It's ideal as a dip base; add pre-mixed seasoning packets or DIY in the spice department. It's also amazing as a sour cream swap, especially if you're sensitive to the taste of fat-free sour cream. A 6-ounce serving of fat-free plain Greek yogurt has about 100 calories. The same amount of low-fat plain Greek yogurt, often labeled 2%, contains about 130 calories and 3 grams of fat.

HG SHOCKER!

If you think the stats on regular whole-milk yogurt are shocking, get this: Full-fat Greek yogurt packs up to **300 calories and 20 grams of fat** per cup! Even scarier? The tubs usually look EXTREMELY similar, so make SURE you grab the ones labeled fat-free, low-fat, 0%, or 2%.

Fat-Free and Low-Fat Greek Yogurt with Fruit

The new wave of fruity Greek yogurts comes in single-serving containers (5 to 6 ounces) with a sidecar of a gooey fruit mixture, and we love this. There are also those that come with a side of honey; these have a good deal more calories, so be careful. Aim for options with 150 calories or so.

HG Tip: If you can't find fruit-ified Greek yogurt, just pick up some sugar-free or low-sugar fruit preserves, and swirl it into your unflavored Greek yogurt. Aren't you resourceful?!

~ PUDDING, DESSERTS, ~ AND DESSERT TOPPINGS

Sugar-Free and No-Sugar-Added Pudding Snack Cups

With 45 to 60 calories, these are almost always lower in calories than their fat-free counterparts. Perfect solo for a sweet fix or as a layered ingredient in pies, parfaits, and more. Chocolate and vanilla are super-common flavors, but seek out more decadent options too, like caramel and even cream pie variations.

HG Snack Tip: Dunk-a-Fruit!
Grab some strawberries and dip 'em in a chocolate snack cup. Plunge some peach slices into vanilla pudding (perhaps zazzled up with a dash of cinnamon)! And if you track down the caramel-flavored pudding cups, it's all about the apple slices . . .

HG FYI:
In addition to instant pudding mix, shelf-stable pudding snacks can be found in the baking aisle. Just remember, the same rules apply: The sugar-free ones give you the best bang for your calorie buck. For more on instant pudding, see page 185 in the Baking Products section.

Snack Cup Cousins!

In addition to classic sugar-free and no-sugar-added pudding, seek out these variations on a theme: mousse (like the 60-calorie Mousse Temptations by Jell-O), rice pudding, and tapioca pudding. Kozy Shack makes the world's best rice and tapioca puddings.

Sugar-Free Gelatin Snack Cups

Hello, **Jell-O**! We can't NOT mention these 10-calorie, sugar-free gelatin snack cups that are always chilling nearby—an ideal treat when you've got to have something sweet but have next-to-no calories left in your daily food budget.

Fat Free Reddi-wip

Weighing in at 5 calories per 2-tablespoon serving, this shake 'n squirt dessert topping is a refrigerator staple. Made with real milk and cream, it has a natural taste to it. It's creamy, it's light, it's airy . . . it's PERFECT. Use it to top beverages (hot or cold), ice cream treats, pudding cups, and parfaits.

That Other Dessert Topping . . . Cool Whip Free!

Head to the freezer aisle and you'll find tubs of fat-free dessert topping, a.k.a. Cool Whip Free. It's a little higher in calories—15 per 2-tablespoon serving—but it's as essential as its 5-calorie counterpart. See **page 142** for more info.

Which One When?
Fat Free Reddi-wip vs. Cool Whip Free

These products are equally valuable, because they serve TOTALLY different purposes. When it comes to topping off anything you plan to devour immediately, it's **Fat Free Reddi-wip** all the way. Think lattes, hot cocoa, blended drinks, and more. For mixing, layering, freezing, and otherwise concocting dessert creations, you need the wonder tub that is **Cool Whip Free**. Think pies, trifles, puddings, and more.

~ EGG PRODUCTS ~

Fat-Free Liquid Egg Substitute

Egg substitute is basically real egg whites with added nutrients and coloring. It comes in a carton with a sealable spout, for easy pouring and storing. A ¼-cup serving, the equivalent of one egg or two egg whites, has 30 calories. The most recognized and best-tasting variety out there is **Egg Beaters Original**. This item can be used practically anywhere real eggs would be used: scrambles, frittatas, omelettes, baked goods, and more. Two unique Hungry Girl uses? Egg mugs and faux-frying. For the full 411 on those, visit Egg-Mug/Egg-Scramble Essentials on page 205 and the Fiber One section on page 24!

Fun Find: If you aren't using egg substitute on the regular, or you just want a fast and pre-measured portion size, seek out individual containers with peel-off lids. These typically come in three-packs, and each pack contains two servings—perfect for a "two-egg scramble" or a recipe calling for two eggs.

Liquid Egg Whites

Truth be told, liquid egg whites are nearly identical to fat-free egg substitute, and the two can almost always be used interchangeably. However, the yellow-hued substitute is better suited for faux-frying (see page 24), where it's used as a binding agent for crumbs and seasoning. Liquid egg whites, on the other hand, are ideal for meringues and recipes where their translucency is valued (dishes where the yellow color would be off-putting).

Eggs

While they're useful for the occasional huevos rancheros or eggs Benedict recipe, whole eggs are a little fat-and-cholesterol-heavy for many people. So why include them in this book? Because hard-boiled egg whites are incredible in recipes and as snacks. They're high in protein and very low in calories. Each large egg white packs only about 17 calories and a whopping 3.5 grams of protein! By the way, each large yolk contains about 55 calories, 4.5 grams of fat, and about 200 milligrams of cholesterol. The choice is yours . . .

HG Snack Tip: Stuff It! Here are some fantastic items to fill your egg-white halves with: fat-free refried beans, salsa, light cheese, Dijon mustard, hummus, tuna, and hot sauce. Mix 'n match! Just don't use them all at once . . .

How to Hard-Boil

Since it's only the whites you're after, you don't really need to be concerned with an exact cooking time or worry about overcooking the eggs. In fact, the more solid the yolks become, the easier it is to separate them from the whites. So, place the eggs in a pot and cover completely with water. The pot should be large enough that there are still a few inches of the pot's inner edge above the water line—this way, the water won't boil over. Bring it to a boil, and then continue to cook for about 10 minutes. After that, carefully drain the water, and cover the eggs in the pot with very cold water. (Got ice? Add it.) Once the eggs are cool enough to handle, crack 'em and the shells should peel off easily. Run a knife along the circumference of each peeled egg to separate the white into halves—like cutting around the pit of an avocado. (It's easier to remove the yolk if you don't slice it in half.) Tada!

~ MILK, MILK SWAPS, ~ AND CREAMERS

⭐ HG All-Star!
Blue Diamond Unsweetened Vanilla Almond Breeze

Consider this the ultimate milk swap. You might be thinking, "Vanilla flavored . . . but not sweetened?! That's ODD!" Trust us: Try it and you'll be hooked. The natural sweetness is enough, and the subtle vanilla taste keeps things flavorful. This all-natural, non-dairy swap is rich, creamy, and tastes FANTASTIC. With just 40 calories per cup, it has less than half as many calories as fat-free milk. It does contain a few grams of fat—3.5 to be exact—and it's worth every one of them. U.V.A.B., as we like to call it, is a tremendously versatile ingredient that's great in most places you'd use milk: cereal bowls, smoothies, coffee drinks, baked goods, and more. And yes, it definitely tastes better than competing unsweetened almond milks.

> **The Where-to-Find 411!** While it is sometimes available in refrigerated cartons, it's typically found in its more popular shelf-stable boxes, stocked with the other non-dairy milk alternatives. It can also be ordered online. If you can't track it down, know that the next item is practically its doppelganger . . .

Light Vanilla Soymilk

Don't assume soymilk is just for the lactose intolerant—if you do, you'll be missing out. Sweet and creamy, light vanilla soymilk is delicious and has fewer calories than regular milk (even the fat-free kind). Look for versions with about 70 calories and 2 grams of fat per cup. Like its fellow milk swap, Unsweetened Vanilla Almond Breeze, this can be useful in nearly all those "I need milk!" moments. Use it in blended beverages, lattes and hot drinks, over cereal, and in baked recipes. The main difference between this and U.V.A.B.? Soymilk is a bit sweeter. So keep that in mind before adding any additional sweetener to whatever you're using it in.

> **A Time and Place for Plain . . .** While vanilla is most useful on a day-to-day basis, plain light soymilk has its purpose too. Use it in creamy soups, savory sauces, and rich dips. Or use it exclusively if you just plain hate vanilla. It's a little lower in calories, with about 60 per cup.

HG FYI: Almond Breeze and light soymilk can be used almost anywhere milk is called for. The exception? With packaged pudding mix. You need old-fashioned fat-free dairy milk for that. (The pudding won't firm up properly with those milk swaps.)

Unsweetened Coconut Milk Beverage

Here's another unconventional milk alternative. With about 50 calories and 5 fat grams per cup, this is light and naturally sugarless. If you're looking for a low-calorie milk swap without soy or almonds, or you just want to infuse some coconutty flavor into your diet, here's a great option for you. It has some fat, but the calorie count is still WAY lower than skim milk. Like Almond Breeze, this can be found in two places: the refrigerated dairy section or the shelf-stable aisle of non-dairy milk swaps.

HG Heads-Up
Don't confuse this dairy-free drink with the thick, creamy goo you get from a can, a.k.a. "lite coconut milk." That has a LOT more fat, is heavily sweetened, and should be used sparingly as a recipe ingredient . . . not sipped straight.

> **HG Standout:** So Delicious. Really, that's the name of the product line. And it is sooooo delicious . . .

Fat-Free Non-Dairy Liquid Creamer

When it comes to flavoring coffee and other drinks with creamy goodness, the liquid kind isn't our first choice. You get the most bang for your calorie buck with the powdered kind. (**More on that in the Coffee, Cocoa, and Tea section on page 174.**) But non-dairy liquid creamer does have its calling. It's ideal as a half & half swap; it tastes better than fat-free half & half. Use it in recipes that need some serious creamy intensity delivered in a small amount of liquid. Mix it into mashed potatoes (we add steamed cauliflower to our mashies!), make super-rich sauces with it, and add it to batters for baked sweets.

HG Heads-Up
Flavored non-dairy liquid creamers—even fat-free ones—typically have TWICE as many calories as the regular unflavored fat-free ones. So be careful! VERY careful . . .

See also . . .

If you're looking for flavored creamer options, flip immediately to page 194! We're all about the powdered kind.

~ SOUR CREAM AND BUTTER ~

Fat-Free Sour Cream

With just 25 calories per 2-tablespoon serving, this is one guilt-free condiment! Use it as a topping for every type of Mexican food imaginable. It's also an amazing blank canvas—it brings a rich and creamy texture with just a touch of tanginess. Use it as a dip base or a sauce starter. Turn something intensely flavored—like spicy salsa, hot mustard, or sweet 'n fruity marinade—into something cool and mild. And if you're not a fan of fat-free mayo, consider using this instead in places that mayo's ordinarily used: scoopable salads (like tuna and chicken), sandwiches, burgers, slaws, and salad dressings. Speaking of salad dressing . . .

HG Dressing Swap!

Bottled fat-free ranch dressing can be less than delicious, but that doesn't mean you can't enjoy ranchy goodness without fat. Whip up your own fat-free ranch dressing by mixing about half a tablespoon of powdered ranch dressing/dip mix (the type that comes in the packets) into ⅓ cup fat-free sour cream; each tablespoon has only 15 calories or so and no fat. And it tastes great—the tanginess of the sour cream works really well with the ranch. Congrats!

Light Buttery Spread and Light Whipped Butter

Look for tubs—not sticks—of these spreadable butters with about 45 calories and 5 grams of fat per tablespoon. That's half as much fat and half as many calories as regular butter. With the spreads, a little goes a long way. And in case you're wondering, yes, there are some fat-free spreads out there with hardly any calories . . . but the light kinds taste SO MUCH BETTER. Try 'em and see!

HG Favorite! Brummel & Brown. It's basically a light buttery spread that's made with yogurt. It tastes just like real butter—maybe a little sweeter. When it comes to light whipped butter, **Land O' Lakes** is our pick.

MYTH-BUSTING WITH HG:

"Shouldn't dieters choose margarine as an alternative to butter?"

Most margarine has just as much fat and just as many calories as regular butter. Some people argue over which is worse: the trans fat in margarine or the saturated fat in butter. We seek out options with less TOTAL fat—like our light whipped butter and light buttery spread picks.

I Can't Believe It's Not Butter! Spray and Other Zero-Calorie-Per-Serving Spray Butters

Zero-calorie butter spray is terrific for day-to-day usage when you only need a few spritzes. In small portions, it's virtually calorie-free, and a little goes a long way. Use it on veggies, on popcorn, and anywhere you need an even mist of buttery goodness. But don't remove the lid and pour! Read on to find out why . . .

HG Heads-Up: The Calorie 411!

Here's the scoop: A single spray has less than a calorie—low enough to be rounded down to zero. If you rack up 10 sprays (½ teaspoon), you're looking at about 10 calories and 1 gram of fat. So, while it isn't exactly "loaded" with calories and fat, it does add up. An entire 8-ounce bottle of spray butter contains around 900 calories and 90 grams of fat. YIKES!

HG Tip: If you tend to go overboard with the spray, you may want to try using a light whipped butter or light buttery spread—the nutritionals are similar, but it's easier to gauge how much you're using and how many calories and fat grams you're taking in.

CEREAL

~ COLD CEREAL ~

HG All-Star!
Fiber One Original Bran Cereal

This is one of the most versatile and indispensable breakfast foods around. These high-fiber cereal twigs are slightly sweet and they taste great. A ½-cup serving has 60 calories, 1 gram of fat, and 14 grams of fiber. It's a great way to give a crunchy fiber boost to yogurt, parfaits, snack mixes, and more. There are other twig-shaped bran cereals with high fiber content, but those aren't as multi-talented as Fiber One Original. So if you plan to use it many different ways, accept no substitutes! Here's what else this miracle ingredient has to offer . . .

Faux-Frying! Fiber One allows us to whip up swaps for fatty fried favorites. Combine it with seasonings in a blender or food processor, and grind to a breadcrumb-like consistency. Lightly coat your food of choice with fat-free liquid egg substitute, and then evenly coat it with the seasoned cereal crumbs. Bake at 375 degrees until cooked through and crunchy, flipping about halfway through bake time, and you've got crispy faux-fried goodies! Try it with skinless lean chicken breast, onions (sliced into rings), shrimp, and eggplant slices.

Fiber Up Your Baked Goods! Crush the stuff and use it in batters, fillings, and so much more. Muffin mixes, pizza crusts, stuffed peppers, and cookie batters!

Pie Crusts! Make a graham-cracker-style crust out of a cup of Fiber One Original, 2 sheets of low-fat graham crackers, 3 tablespoons of granulated no-calorie sweetener, and ¼ cup light whipped butter or light buttery spread. Just grind the cereal and crackers to crumbs and mix with sweetener. Melt the butter with 2 tablespoons of water, and mix with sweetened crumbs. Press it all into a pie pan sprayed with nonstick spray, and bake until firm, about 10 minutes at 350 degrees. Each serving of the resulting crust (⅛th) will have 55 calories, 3 grams of fat, and 3.5 grams of fiber.

Crunchy Salad Topper! It's the ultimate slightly sweet crouton swap for salads. It's especially good on Chinese chicken salads and fruity salads.

! CALORIE BARGAIN ALERT!
Puffed Grains (Unsweetened)

In terms of cereal PORTIONS, these give you the best bang for your calorie buck. They're made by expanding the grain kernels with air pressure—a process similar to popping corn. Have a cup of the super-light and airy stuff for just about 60 calories. Look for rice, wheat, and corn varieties. Though not nutritional powerhouses, these are GREAT for bulking up cereal bowls and snack mixes.

HG Tip: It's in the Bag . . . You'll often find these puffs packaged in plastic bags as opposed to standard boxes. Good to know . . .

What About Sweetened? While it isn't nearly as low in calories as its no-sugar-added counterparts, sweetened puffed cereal is delicious and pretty reasonable. A cup of it tends to have around 120 calories.

GENERAL CEREAL GUIDELINES:

 Look for options with 150 calories and 2 grams of fat or less per 1-cup serving. (Of course, if you find a higher-calorie cereal you love that fits into your diet and satisfies you, go for it!)

 More fiber usually means a cereal will help keep you feeling full—our favorites have 4 grams of fiber or more per serving.

 Seek out cereal with protein. Like fiber, protein is filling. Those with the highest counts are usually made with wheat, oats, and other whole grains.

Super-Important Serving-Size Info!
A serving of dry cereal can range anywhere from ¼ cup to 2 cups. So if you're comparing calorie counts and other stats, pay close attention to serving-size measurements.

Ginormous Cereal Bowl Alert!

Mixing a ton of puffed cereal with a serving of Fiber One Original will give you a HUGE and FIBER-PACKED cereal bowl with a totally reasonable calorie count. Top it off with your milk or milk swap of choice (see the Dairy section) and some fruit (freeze-dried or fresh). If you're craving some decadent cereal you'd rather not spend too many calories on, adding a small amount to this bowl is a great way to get your fix!

Cereal Shape Shakedown

Here's the full 411 on some other cereal types . . .

Flakes — Light and super-crunchy, these are usually a good option. Corn and bran are most common. A cup of corn flakes has about 100 calories, 2 grams of protein, and 1 gram of fiber. The average cup of bran flakes contains 140 calories, 3 grams of protein, and 5 grams of fiber.

O's — Circle-shaped cereal is crunchy and pretty common. And in case you're wondering, the O usually stands for oats. These aren't very light, but they're not too dense either. A 1-cup serving packs in about 110 calories, 3 grams of protein, and 3 grams of fiber.

Shredded — Almost always made from wheat, but sometimes oats. Delicious and definitely satiating, with about 5 grams each of fiber and protein per serving. But know that a 1-cup serving has about 180 calories, which is higher than many other cereals.

Clusters — These tend to be dense and consist of pieces of fruit and nuts fused with grains. Stats vary in this category. A cup of clusters often contains anywhere from 160 to 220 calories, 4 to 8 grams of protein, and 4 to 10 grams of fiber.

HG Standouts: Kashi makes amazing all-natural cereals that are high in fiber and taste delicious. Fiber One has some decadent cereals that are infused with fiber (unlike many sweet cereals on shelves). With any brand, just check the cereal's calorie count to make sure it suits your needs. And remember to mix 'n match the lighter varieties with the more indulgent stuff!

Kid Classics: The Sweet Stuff

If you crave chocolate, peanut butter, marshmallows, and fruity crunch, you could do a lot worse than some of the retro cereals on shelves. Compared to cookies, pastries, and candy bars, this can be a reasonable way to get a sweet fix. Have it dry as a snack, add a little to your cereal bowl of healthier picks, use it as a dessert or yogurt topping. You can even blend it into smoothies and use it in dessert recipes.

Single-Serving Alert! Don't discount those mini boxes. With 70 to 120 calories each, they're perfect for stashing at the office, in your car, in a backpack . . . Even if you don't have access to milk, they can be a great emergency snack straight out of the box.

HG SHOCKER!

Even Low-Fat Granola Contains Close to 400 Calories per Cup!
Granola may be filled with nutrient-dense stuff, but if you're counting calories and fat, the stats add up FAST. A mere ½-cup serving has about 210 calories! And it's one of the few cereal types that contains a LOT of fat; each serving has an average of 6 grams . . . and remember, that's for only HALF A CUP! Don't be fooled into thinking that low-fat granola is much lower in calories, because it isn't. Despite its lower fat count, expect to spend 190 calories on a ½-cup serving.

~ HOT CEREAL ~

* NEED-TO-KNOW LINGO *
OATS EDITION

Oats are high-fiber whole grains with a heart-healthy reputation. Here's a quick rundown of the different types of oats on shelves . . .

Instant
Precooked oats can be prepped in as little as a minute, either in the microwave or by adding boiling water. They are the thinnest of the bunch, with less natural flavor and texture than other kinds.

Quick-Cooking
Oats that have been rolled thin and cut into smaller pieces, yielding a cook time of just a couple of minutes.

Old-Fashioned
Oat flakes that have been steamed, pressed, and toasted. Minimally processed for maximum health benefits. These are like the happy medium of the oat world. Hearty without an exhaustive cook time.

Steel-Cut (Irish)
Coarse, chopped-up oats. These take the longest to cook, about 30 minutes, but yield oatmeal with the most texture and flavor. While the dry serving size is half the measurement of the others, once cooked it yields the same amount as other oats.

Old-Fashioned Oats

Eat something loaded with rolled oats, and you'll likely feel full for a good long time. Plus, these oats can soak up a whole lotta liquid, and foods with high water content lead to maximum satisfaction. A ½-cup serving (dry) has about 150 calories, 3 grams of fat, 4 grams of fiber, and 5 grams of protein.

Supersize It! Cooked the regular way, a serving yields one cup. But we like to cook our oats for two to three times as long (about 15 minutes) with twice as much liquid (a cup of water plus a cup of Unsweetened Vanilla Almond Breeze)—the result is a gigantic serving of creamy and delicious oatmeal.

Think Outside the Cereal Bowl . . . We enjoy putting oats in places they wouldn't ordinarily go, like pancakes, pizza crusts, and dessert recipes. Not only can they add nice subtle texture, but they can also up the fiber count of whatever you're consuming. (Oats are like fiber ninjas!)

Instant Oatmeal Packets

These are your best bet when you're in a hurry, and they're convenient to stash in workplaces, dorm rooms, desk drawers, etc. Just add boiling water or prepare in the microwave for a hot breakfast or anytime snack. They've also got the portion-control thing going for them, but a serving is on the small side, so we often have two packets at a time. The average packet (about an ounce) of plain has 100 calories, 2 grams of fat, 3 grams of fiber, and 4 grams of protein. Flavored types have about 150 calories per packet.

Fun Flavor Alert! While your basic apple cinnamon and maple spice options are delicious, sometimes you want to get a little crazy. When that happens, look for the kid-targeted or pastry-inspired varieties—like chocolate chip, banana bread, and cinnamon bun. Just keep an eye on those calorie and sugar counts.

Sugar Savers and Fiber Boosters for Flavor Cravers: If you love flavored oatmeal but not all the sugar that comes along with it, seek out those labeled "lower sugar." These have about 5 grams of sugar; regular flavored packets usually have at least twice that. Fiber fans can find "high-fiber" packets of flavored oatmeal with about 40 percent of the daily value of fiber, 10 grams. Not bad!

MEAT & SEAFOOD

MEAT & SEAFOOD

Boneless Skinless Lean Chicken Breast and Turkey Breast

These are two of the most versatile and diet-friendly types of meat out there. High in protein and low in calories and fat. Check out your options for both raw and cooked selections . . .

* Raw — Buy it raw and cook it yourself for the least amount of sodium. It's often sold in several forms, including whole breasts, cutlets, and tenders. The smaller the pieces, the more quickly they'll cook.

* Precooked — Buy it precooked for the convenience factor. In addition to whole breasts, ready-to-eat chicken can often be found chopped or as strips—these are the most convenient, since you can easily add them to salads, wraps, and more. But the precooked kind is often high in sodium, so read labels if you're a sodium counter.

What About Wings and Drumsticks?
Skip the Skin and Save!

While the stats on the packages are pretty high, a good portion of fat and calories comes from the skin. Remove the skin to reduce those counts. A small skinless wing (about 1 ounce, uncooked) has about 40 calories and 1 gram of fat—the same-sized wing with skin contains about 60 calories and 4.5 grams of fat. A standard drumstick with the skin removed (2 ounces, uncooked) has 75 calories and 2 grams of fat—the skin-on, 2-ounce stick has about 120 calories and 6 grams of fat.

Pssst . . .

Poultry lovers should check out the Shelf-Stable Seafood and Other Proteins section for info about an unexpected find—canned chicken!

Lean Ground Turkey

While extra-lean ground turkey is an option, it can be a little dry and tasteless. The lean kind is flavorful and still reasonable in stats. Look for options with about 160 calories and 8 grams of fat per 4-ounce uncooked serving. Use it for homemade meatballs, chili, and thick 'n hearty sauces. Fun tip? Mix the lean with the extra-lean . . .

Lean Turkey Burger Patties

Found in both freezer aisles and fridge sections, these burgers are lean ground turkey portioned out and flattened into patties. Sometimes they're seasoned with salt and other spices. Choose these if you're not a fan of working with ground meat, but opt for unseasoned lean ground turkey for more control over the taste and salt content.

HG Heads-Up
There are many non-lean turkey burgers out there; those have significantly more fat. Look for lean patties with about 160 calories and 8 grams of fat each.

Lean Turkey Sausage

Find fully cooked links and patties in both the refrigerated and freezer sections. They're almost always lean, but they *don't* always have the word stamped across the front, so you might have to read a few nutritional panels to find the lean options. Breakfast links are small, typically an ounce each, and have about 45 calories and 3 grams of fat per link. They usually come in servings of two or three. The patties and larger links have similar serving weights and stats per ounce, with 2 patties or 1 link per serving. So regardless of size, seek out those with 140 calories and 9 grams of fat or less per 3-ounce serving. Some are higher in stats and larger in size, so read those labels.

HG Heads-Up
Be sure to check out the Meat Substitutes section for guilt-free and delicious vegetarian options.

Turkey Pepperoni

This lower-fat alternative to real pepperoni tastes almost exactly like the real thing. There are a few brands on shelves, but **Hormel** has the best, hands down. Have a 17-slice serving for just 70 calories and 4 grams of fat . . . That's a LOT of pepperoni! These are a great way to make anything taste like pizza. Try slathering some chicken in pizza sauce and topping it with part-skim mozzarella and a few of these slices. AWESOME!

> See the Bacon section for the 411 on turkey bacon!

Extra-Lean Ground Beef

Unlike extra-lean ground turkey, extra-lean ground beef isn't dry at all. Look for packages with around 140 calories and 4.5 grams of fat per 4-ounce uncooked serving. Extra-lean ground beef is usually labeled as having 4 percent fat. Like lean ground turkey, it can be used in tons of recipes: taco meat, burger patties, meatloaf, and more.

Extra-Lean and Lean Steak

Cuts of beef that fit the bill for extra-lean status are top round and top sirloin. Lean kinds include strip, tenderloin, T-bone, and shoulder. Our picks are top sirloin and tenderloin.

Raw Meat Selection & Preparation 101

Look for those with the least amount of visible fat (the white marbling). Of these options, seek out ones where the fat is grouped together as opposed to spread out in thin ribbons—this makes excess fat easier to remove. Speaking of which, when preparing to cook, trim as much of the fat from the meat as possible. Using a designated set of kitchen shears is much less difficult than going at it with a knife!

HG Tip: When cooking raw meat, a small amount of salt and pepper goes a long way in terms of enhancing its flavor. If you prefer to cook without salt, opt for other spices like garlic and onion powder.

~ PORK ~

Extra-Lean and Lean Pork

Many cuts have as little as 3 to 6 grams of fat per serving. Cuts with the word "loin" or "round" in the name are the leanest. Pork tenderloin is extra-lean, and the lean varieties are boneless top loin chops, boneless top loin roast, center loin chops, center rib chops, and bone-in sirloin roast. But here's a great tip when you want to whip up pulled pork with much less fat than the standard kind made with pork shoulder (which has a high fat content): Use equal parts sensible tenderloin and decadent shoulder (both trimmed of excess fat). Once slow cooked, shredded, and combined, your pork will have delicious flavor with completely reasonable stats!

Guilt-Free Shocker Alert!

With about **120 calories** and **3 grams of fat** per 3.5-ounce uncooked serving, pork tenderloin is as low in calories as skinless chicken breast. WOW.

* NEED-TO-KNOW LINGO * MEAT EDITION

Lean
A 3.5-ounce serving of lean meat contains no more than 10 grams of fat. Often labeled as being at least 93% fat-free or as having 7 percent fat or less.

Extra-Lean
A serving of 3.5 ounces of extra-lean meat has 5 grams of fat or less. Also marked as anywhere from 96% to 99% fat-free or containing no more than 4 percent fat.

Lower-Sodium/Less-Sodium/Reduced-Sodium
At least 25 percent less sodium than a standard product.

Low-Sodium
No more than 140 milligrams per serving.

Center-Cut Bacon and Turkey Bacon

When it comes to pork bacon, center-cut is your best bet. It's sliced close to the bone, so it's less fatty than the standard stuff. When it comes to turkey bacon, no need to skimp on taste and texture with the extra-lean versions—traditional turkey bacon is lean and tastes great. A slice of either of these has about 30 calories and 2.5 grams of fat.

HG Tip: Drain and discard bacon drippings to cut the fat count. Or cook it in the microwave, and let a few paper towels soak up any excess grease.

HG Heads-Up
Watch out for "thick-cut" bacon, which can contain twice the calories and fat of standard cuts.

Precooked Real Crumbled Bacon

Craving bacon but too time-crunched to break out a skillet? Imitation bacon's not your only option. Precooked real crumbled bacon in sealable bags can often be found right next to the fake bacon (usually in the salad dressing aisle). With about 25 calories and 1.5 grams of fat per tablespoon, it's similar in stats to center-cut and turkey bacon. It's more moist than the crispy imitation bacon and perfect for adding almost anywhere you'd use chopped bacon: salads, soups, scrambles, main dishes, and more. Score!

Imitation Bacon Bits

Made from textured soy protein, these aren't a bad option at all. A tablespoon has about 20 calories and 1 gram of fat. These are crispier and crunchier than crumbled bacon, and they've got a longer shelf life. Heads up, though: They're not always completely vegetarian-friendly, so read ingredient labels carefully if that's a concern.

Canadian Bacon

Deli meat, meet breakfast! Canadian bacon is naturally lean and great as a b-fast sandwich component or morning meal side. A 2-ounce serving packs about 70 calories and 2.5 grams of fat. Like regular deli ham, it's high in sodium, so skip it or limit it if you're watching your salt.

~ PACKAGED AND DELI MEATS ~

Guilt-Free Shocker Alert!

Not only is roast beef decadent and delicious, it's also readily available in extra-lean! So if you're craving Arby's, stock up on this stuff instead.

Extra-Lean Turkey Breast, Chicken Breast, Ham, and Roast Beef Slices

These are great for more than just sandwiches. Roll them around pickle spears, pile them on top of high-fiber crackers, and snack on them straight. If you don't see the words extra-lean, look for at least 96% fat-free. The average 2-ounce serving (about 4 to 6 slices) contains 50 to 60 calories and 1 to 2 grams of fat. Shaved and ultra-thin kinds give you the most slices per serving, while thickly cut varieties have fewer slices per serving. And don't discount the deli counter by only buying packaged slices. Depending on the store and your exact needs, the deli can offer better selection and price. So check both places before you buy!

Salt-Slashing 411: If salt's a concern, seek out no-salt-added and lower-salt options. You may find those more readily available at the deli counter. Or DIY—cook your own meat and slice it yourself.

HG All-Natural Picks: If you prefer to keep things natural and avoid antibiotics, hormones, and preservatives, there are deli-style choices for you. Applegate and Boar's Head All Natural are two types worth seeking out.

~ HOT DOGS ~

97% to 100% Fat-Free Hot Dogs

There are so many options for frankfurters with about 40 calories and 1 gram of fat each. Hoffy Extra Lean Beef Franks (hard to find but worth it) and Hebrew National 97% Fat Free Beef Franks (easy to locate and incredible!) are two Hungry Girl favorites. If beef's not your thing, there are great-tasting chicken and turkey options out there; we like the kinds by Applegate and Ball Park. And don't think you need to be bound by a bun. Franks are great in wraps, salads, soups, scrambles, and even chili!

HG SHOCKER!

All chicken and turkey dogs are NOT created equal. Many contain as much—if not MORE fat—than regular full-fat beef hot dogs. So read labels carefully!

~ SEAFOOD ~

Tilapia, Tuna, and Other Lean Fillets

Tilapia's a great blank slate; it's mild with a nice light texture. It's also one of the lowest-calorie fish, with about 110 calories and 2 grams of fat per 4-ounce uncooked portion, and it's practically all protein. Tuna is heartier, almost steak-like—choose sushi-grade and you can enjoy it raw, seared, or fully cooked. Yellowfin's the most common, and it has about 120 calories and 1 gram of fat per 4-ounce uncooked serving. Other types of fresh lean fish? Cod, snapper, and flounder. Those have stats similar to tilapia and tuna.

Salmon

Usually Atlantic or Alaskan, salmon's a fatty fish—a 4-ounce serving, raw, has about 200 calories and 12 grams of fat—but it's loaded with omega-3 fatty acids, a.k.a. good-for-you fat. So pair it with light sides and sauces to keep calories and fat in check.

Lox-Style Smoked Salmon: It doesn't get much more convenient than this stuff. It's delicious chilled, right out of the fridge. The sodium count is fairly high—about 780 milligrams per 2-ounce serving—but a little goes a long way since it's so thinly sliced. This is a great staple for a quick protein fix with "good" fats!

Shrimp

Simply put, shrimp rocks. High in protein and low in calories, with about 100 calories and 1 gram of fat per 4-ounce uncooked serving. Lots of options here—from small to jumbo, fresh to frozen, tail-on and unshelled to peeled and ready-to-eat. Fresh, ready-to-eat tastes the best, but it's also the priciest. The least expensive is frozen and needs to be peeled, cleaned, deveined, and cooked. A happy medium? Opt for peeled and deveined frozen raw shrimp. You do have to thaw and cook it, but the hard work is done for you.

What's the Deal with Counts per Pound?

In short? The higher the number per pound, the smaller the shrimp. In long? See the nifty chart!

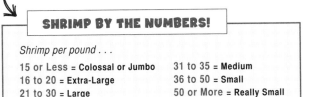

SHRIMP BY THE NUMBERS!

Shrimp per pound . . .

15 or Less = **Colossal or Jumbo**	31 to 35 = **Medium**
16 to 20 = **Extra-Large**	36 to 50 = **Small**
21 to 30 = **Large**	50 or More = **Really Small**

Scallops

A fun change from shrimp, scallops are delicious and low in calories. A 4-ounce uncooked serving contains about 100 calories and 1 gram of fat. Like shrimp, these range from small (bay scallops) to super-large (sea scallops).

Crab

Like the other shellfish in this section, crab is full of protein and low in fat. A serving of 4 ounces (cooked, which is how it's most often sold) has about 115 calories and 2 grams of fat. Crab legs can be expensive and are high in sodium, but they taste great. Finding decent packaged crabmeat can be tricky—some kinds taste too "fishy." So once you find a kind you love, stick with it! Our reasonably priced pick? Chicken of the Sea Lump Crab. There are other options that taste INCREDIBLE (Trade Winds and MeTompkin), but those are super-pricey and best for special occasions.

What's the Deal with Imitation Crabmeat?

Imitation crab is made of minced pollock (a mild white fish) that's blended with other ingredients—like sugar, sorbitol, wheat, and egg whites—to mimic crab's natural texture. It's a little sweeter and less fishy than real crab, with a firmer texture.

↓

3 ounces (uncooked)	Real Crab	Fake Crab
Calories:	80	80
Fat:	1 gram	1 gram
Sodium:	500 milligrams	600 milligrams
Carbs:	0 grams	11 grams
Protein:	15 grams	7 grams
Cost:	Can Be Pricey	Moderate
Taste:	Varies	Consistent
Convenience:	Sometimes	Always

↓

The Verdict?

Both have their time, place, and purpose. Real crab can be fresh tasting and delicious but also a little expensive. It's best savored solo or with minimal add-ons. Imitation crab has its own flavor—which is unique and delicious. It's usually a bargain and almost always easy to work with. Fake crab is perfect for all sorts of recipes: cheesy ones, creamy ones, hot ones, cold ones. Crabulous!

Canned and Pouched Albacore Tuna Packed in Water

Two great options, both high in protein and low in calories and fat. Choose pouches as a convenient snack you can stash anywhere you might need a protein pick-me-up. You don't need a can opener and you don't need to drain them. Cans are great for recipes and most at-home assembly. And don't think fat-free mayo and celery are your only mix-in options. Get creative with mustard, sauces, salad dressings, salsa . . . even fruit, like crushed pineapple packed in juice.

> **Salt-Slashing 411:** Opting for low-sodium tuna saves about 150mg of sodium per 2-ounce serving.

TUNA LABEL FAQS:

What's the difference between chunk and solid?

These terms have to do with the way the tuna is canned and how flaky it is. Chunk is flakier, so use it when you plan to mix it up with other ingredients. Solid is heartier and won't fall apart, so choose that when you want to plunge your fork into something sturdy (and when it's on sale!). Solid is more expensive and higher in quality.

What about white versus light tuna?

White tuna refers to pure albacore. Light tuna is a combo of tuna types, like bluefin and yellowfin. The light kind will save you a small amount of fat and calories, but all-albacore white tuna is top quality in terms of taste.

Is oil-packed tuna really that much higher in fat?

In a word? YES. Unlike some items packed in oil, like sun-dried tomatoes, you can't effectively avoid consuming all the excess oil. It really soaks in and sticks. Even "light" tuna packed in oil has about 120 calories and 5 grams of fat per 2-ounce serving. A 2-ounce serving of albacore tuna packed in water contains around 70 calories and 1 gram of fat. Stick with tuna packed in water.

Canned and Pouched Boneless and Skinless Pink Salmon Packed in Water

This pink precooked protein is very different from the red-hued fillets that come fresh or frozen. A 3-ounce serving has about 120 calories and 5 grams of fat, and it's a nice source of those healthy omega-3s. The taste is mild, and you can use this stuff pretty much anywhere you'd use tuna.

HG Heads-Up

Watch out for the meal kits in this aisle. They might seem like a good idea, but they're often filled with things you don't want or need, like crackers, cheese, and packets of fatty mayo.

Pouched Seasoned Tuna and Salmon

Smarter choices than prepared deli salads, these tend to be nicely flavored with sauces and spices rather than weighed down with mayo. There are many flavor options, from fruity to fiery. And the stats are usually very good; just check the labels carefully. The Creations line by StarKist is pretty impressive in our book. (And this is our book.)

Pouched Ready-to-Serve Seasoned Albacore and Salmon Steak Fillets

These are FUN! You might be skeptical of the whole meal-in-a-shelf-stable-bag thing. We get it, really. We're still not fans of ready-to-eat, shelf-stable chicken-breast pouches. But the fish folks have really mastered these flavored fillets. These can be GREAT toppers for fast-food salads ordered on the fly. Instant protein! Look for those under 200 calories and with about 5 grams of fat each—good stats for their size.

Canned 98% Fat-Free Chunk White Chicken Breast in Water

Seems a little scary at first, but it works great in recipes, especially for Mexican food. Mix it with salsa, BBQ sauce, cheese, or taco seasoning, and you've got super-fast family-friendly food. Don't be afraid to swap out the canned tuna in a favorite recipe, like tuna salad or an open-faced melt. Try something new . . . do it! Each 2-ounce serving (about ¼ cup) has 60 calories or so and 1 gram of fat.

Meat 'n Seafood by the Numbers . . .

Read up, Hungry!

4 ounces (uncooked)	Calories	Fat
Skinless chicken breast	125	2 grams
Skinless turkey breast	125	1 gram
Lean ground turkey	160	8 grams
Extra-lean ground beef	140	4.5 grams
Extra-lean steak	150	4.5 grams
Lean steak	175	8 grams
Extra-lean pork	140	4 grams
Lean pork	185	10 grams
Tilapia	110	2 grams
Tuna	120	1 gram
Atlantic salmon	205	12 grams
Shrimp	100	1 gram
Scallops	100	1 gram
Crab	100	1 gram

MEAT SUBSTITUTES

Frozen Meatless Hamburger-Style Patties

These freezer-aisle items are great alternatives to real beef burgers. Most are made from soy and pack a hearty, super-savory grilled taste. Like real burgers, they're high in protein; but unlike beef, these are low in fat and typically pack in some fiber as an added bonus. Look for patties with about 100 calories each. You can prepare 'em in the microwave if you're in a hurry, but they taste best cooked in a skillet, in a grill pan, or on the grill.

⭐ HG All-Star!

Boca Original Vegan Meatless Burgers! These have an impressively low 70 calories each, and they're some of the best-tasting soy patties around.

Also Great: Options by Amy's and Morningstar Farms! Specifically, Amy's Bistro Burgers and Morningstar Farms Grillers Vegan Veggie Burgers. Delicious, guilt-free goodness.

Secret Swap! Looking for a fast ground meat substitute? Just cook, cool, and crumble into small pieces!

Frozen Meatless Veggie-Burger Patties

Veggie burgers are usually jam-packed with chopped vegetables (like onions, zucchini, mushrooms, and bell peppers), grains (rice, oats, etc.) and, sometimes, cheese. There are plenty of 100-calorie-or-less options to choose from. They're high in fiber like burger-style patties, but they tend to be a little lower in protein. Cook 'em up just like their soy-based counterparts: mega-fast in the microwave or patiently in a skillet (or grill pan) or on a grill.

The Best and Original: Gardenburger The Original Veggie Burgers. Three types of mushrooms, two types of cheese, brown rice, and rolled oats . . . all perfectly seasoned and pressed into patty form. Love these! GB's other varieties are also delicious.

Extra, Extra!

Don't miss the Burger Essentials section on page 202!

Which One When?
Hamburger-Style Patties vs. Veggie-Burger Patties

Hamburger-style patties are like the little black dress of patty parties (except for the fact that they're brown and shaped like Frisbees). Just add the appropriate accessories—ketchup, relish, and mustard for a classic burger; teriyaki sauce and a pineapple ring for an island-inspired burger fix; sautéed onion and guilt-free cheese for a patty melt . . . whatever! Use them to re-create your dream hamburger for far fewer fat grams and calories. Veggie-burger patties bring more of their own distinctive flavor and texture to the table in every bite; it doesn't take much to zazzle 'em up. Try one crisply cooked and chopped over spinach leaves with light honey mustard dressing. Slice one into strips and toss into a wrap with a few veggies and a little Dijonnaise. Mmmmm! One place they both go equally well? Backyard BBQs, or anyplace else with a grill!

Frozen Ground-Beef-Style Soy Crumbles

Aliases: Boca Meatless Ground Crumbles and Morningstar Farms Meal Starters Grillers Recipe Crumbles

Not sure what these are? We'll tell you. They're meat-like textured veggie protein crumbles, and they're chilling out in the freezer aisle. They're seasoned well enough to taste good but lightly enough so that they work well in whatever you're whipping up. Not only is this stuff lower in calories and fat than most ground meats, but it's also perfect for use in recipes that require small quantities of meat. Does your snack or meal need a protein boost? Add a scoop of soy crumbles! They can be heated in the microwave, cooked in a skillet, and even added straight to stovetop recipes. The best part? No browning, crumbling, or draining required!

A Meat for All Seasons . . .

Add Italian spices and a little reduced-fat Parmesan, and you're on your way to a meaty pasta sauce. Toss in taco seasoning and taco sauce, and you've got Mexican taco meat! Add some cheese, veggies, and a casserole dish, and it's American-style family food!

Serving-Size Conundrum . . . If you glance briefly at the nutritional panels of Boca Meatless Ground Crumbles and Morningstar Farms Meal Starters Grillers Recipe Crumbles, it seems like Morningstar's version has more calories. But check out the serving sizes, and then compare the nutritionals cup for cup. Morningstar's version actually has the same amount of calories as Boca's. And now you know!

Ground-Beef-Style Soy Crumbles (4 oz. frozen) =
140 calories, 2.5g fat, 500mg sodium, 11g carbs, 5g fiber,
0.5g sugars, 17g protein

Extra-Lean Ground Beef (4 oz. uncooked) =
140 calories, 4.5g fat, 80mg sodium, 0g carbs, 0g fiber,
0g sugars, 24g protein

Lean Ground Turkey (4 oz. uncooked) =
160 calories, 8g fat, 90mg sodium, 0g carbs, 0g fiber,
0g sugars, 22g protein

HG Heads-Up

Keep in mind, while the crumbles contain more sodium than regular
ground meat, they're already seasoned (unlike the others). Adding
even a few dashes of salt to either of the meats while cooking
increases their counts to about 500 milligrams of sodium as well.

Meatless Meatballs
(Frozen and Refrigerated)

These aren't as readily available on shelves as burger patties or
even crumbles, but they're worth seeking out. Even if you do
eat meat, these can be a fantastic alternative to beef and turkey
meatballs, both of which can be high in fat and calories. Look for
meatless options with about 110 calories and 4.5 grams of fat per
3-ounce serving (3 to 6 meatballs). Like most meat alternatives,
they pack a few grams of fiber and an impressive amount of protein,
usually about a dozen grams of protein per serving.

Time to Get Saucy . . . These are delicious sauced up
with seasoned crushed tomatoes or low-fat marinara sauce. Opt
for stovetop cooking rather than the microwave, so the sauce can
really soak in.

MEAT SUBSTITUTES

Frozen Meatless Sausage-Style Breakfast Patties and Links

Another great alternative, even for meat eaters. A serving of traditional breakfast sausage (1 patty or 2 links) often contains at least 150 calories and 10 grams of fat. And remember, breakfast sausage is small. The meatless types have just 80 calories and 3 grams of fat or so per patty or 2-link serving. The patties are perfect for breakfast sandwiches; just put a cooked patty on a light English muffin along with a slice of fat-free American cheese and some scrambled fat-free egg substitute. But also, get creative—chop 'em up to yield sausage crumbles, and then use those to make pizza, lasagna, and more! The links are ideal for serving alongside egg scrambles and other hot breakfast bites!

Refrigerated Soy Chorizo, a.k.a. Soyrizo

This is the meatless version of chorizo, a beloved spicy Mexican/Spanish sausage. It's dark reddish-brown and comes encased in a cylinder of clear plastic so it *looks* like an actual sausage. This flavorful swap has a fraction of the fat and calories of its pork-based inspiration. A 2-ounce serving has around 100 calories and 7 grams of fat. Cooked and crumbled in a hot skillet until browned and slightly crispy, a little goes a long way! Use to inject savory Mexican spice into omelettes, scrambles, soups, and chili. Mmmmm . . .

HG SHOCKER!

> A 2-ounce serving of real chorizo has about 250 calories and 20 grams of fat. Eeeeks!

Where to Find:
Frozen and Refrigerated

Meat swaps are found in both the freezer and fridge sections of the market. The freezer-aisle items are often easier to track down and are all found in one area. Look for the section labeled Vegetarian, Meatless, Veggie Burgers, Meat Alternatives, or Soy Products. Refrigerated meat substitutes can be a bit trickier. If the previously mentioned labels aren't present in the fridge section, look in the tofu section or check the place where the "real" versions are stocked. When in doubt, ask a friendly stock boy . . .

ATE GREAT Brands
in the Meat-Swapping Arena . . .

1. **Boca** (soy patties & crumbles!)
2. **Morningstar Farms** (crumbles & corn dogs!)
3. **Amy's** (everything!)
4. **Gardenburger** (veggie burgers!)
5. **Lightlife** (wings!)
6. **Veggie Patch** (meatballs!)
7. **Nate's** (more meatballs!)
8. **Dr. Praeger's** (veggie burgers . . . blot the oil!)

Faux Grilled Chicken Patties, Cutlets, and Strips (Frozen and Refrigerated)

These chicken swaps can be used practically anywhere actual cooked poultry is used: salads, sandwiches, recipes, etc. Look for versions that are low in fat with 80 to 100 calories per serving, like the kinds by Boca and Morningstar Farms. And when in doubt, go with the brands you know you love—if you like their soy patties, chances are their faux chicken will make you happy too!

Frozen Breaded-Chicken-Style Soy Patties

Here's a product that makes our jobs easy and cravings easier to handle. Breaded chicken is mostly off-limits when it comes to dining out or on the go. A fast-food chicken sandwich typically has more than 500 calories and 25 grams of fat! Make your own at-home swap with one of these, a light hamburger bun, and some fat-free mayo. Your chicken sandwich will have less than half the calories and a quarter of the fat of similar fast-food versions. These patties also taste great chopped up and added to salads or wrapped up in high-fiber tortillas. Or slice one up, and eat it as is. See ya later, chicken fingers. Look for options with about 150 calories and 6 grams of fat each.

Meatless Meats FYI: They're Timesavers!

These rarely come "raw"—they're often fully or partially cooked and require less cook time than real meat. Hooray for that!

~ MEATLESS NOVELTIES ~

Corn Dogs, Wings, Nuggets & More (Frozen and Refrigerated)

These are decadent swaps for fattening favorites. Even meat-loving calorie counters will appreciate their delicious taste and impressively low fat and calorie counts . . . A few brands make corn dogs, most notably Morningstar Farms. These served-on-a-stick meatless treats are (almost) as good as the state-fair grease bombs, but with about 75 percent less fat (only 3 grams total). Buffalo wings and chicken nuggets come courtesy of several brands as well, including a few refrigerated products. But the stats can vary vastly, so browse around before you buy. Seek out versions with no more than 200 calories per serving. The mac daddy of meatless novelties may very well be Morningstar Farms Hickory BBQ Riblets, a.k.a. the ultimate swap for McDonald's McRib sandwich. The saucy soy riblet has lots of fiber and protein, and is fairly low in calories (220). All of these are fantastic ways to feed a craving for the real fat-filled thing!

A word about meatless deli slices and hot dogs . . . We have to admit—a disappointing category. We've tried many, and as much as we want to like them, we haven't found any that truly taste good. If you avoid beef but enjoy turkey and chicken, we strongly recommend that you check out turkey dogs and chicken dogs . . . Those we like.

See also . . .

The Packaged Snacks section for meatless jerky and the Meat & Seafood section for the 411 on imitation bacon bits!

MEAT SUBSTITUTES

PRODUCE

PRODUCE

HG's Favorite Veggies
from Artichokes to Zucchini

We're going veggie crazy—in alphabetical order! Browse through or flip around for info. If you ever get overwhelmed in the produce aisle and wish you had more info on those fresh finds, here's the 411 . . .

Artichokes
60 calories and 7 grams of fiber per artichoke

Don't be scared of their pointiness . . . Artichokes rock! The trick is to STEAM them—don't cook them in a ton of oil like most restaurants. Then dip the leaves in light sauces: Try melted light butter mixed with lemon juice, salsa mixed with fat-free sour cream, or straight-up salsa.

Asparagus
25 calories and 3 grams of fiber for 8 spears

Here's a real superstar of spring. Asparagus is great in that it tastes terrific, seems kinda fancy and special, and is chock-full of nutrients. To prep these stalks, just bend them until the tough ends snap off. Discard those ends and you're ready to cook. Steam or boil them for soft spears, or grill them lightly for a hearty crunch.

Bell Peppers: Red, Green, Yellow, and Orange
30 calories and 2 grams of fiber per pepper

Use assorted colors for stir-frys, fajitas, scrambles, omelettes, and pizza-esque dishes. The sweeter ones—red, yellow, and orange—are great for slicing and snacking on straight. Big fan of potato skins? Try making bell pepper skins; just use shredded fat-free or reduced-fat cheese, precooked real crumbled bacon, and chopped scallions. SO GOOD!

Broccoli

30 calories and 2.5 grams of fiber per cup

Broccoli florets bring fiber and crunch to the table. They rock in the wok (or skillet) for stir-frys. They take a little longer to cook than veggies cut into strips, so start 'em early and add a little liquid. Or chop 'em up for a faster cook time. Steam it and toss it with leftover Chinese food. There's usually enough sauce to go around, and it tastes great with everything from garlic chicken to shrimp with lobster sauce. Use it to fill out saucy frozen dinners too! Broccoli's also awesome as a snack . . . Try it with salsa!

See also . . . Broccoli cole slaw mix, in the Best Bagged Produce section. It's another Supersizing Superstar!

Brussels Sprouts

40 calories and 3.5 grams of fiber per cup

These baby cabbages are totally underrated. Roast 'em and they take on a rich, caramelized flavor. Just be careful not to overcook 'em. (If you do, they'll start to smell funny and develop a wilty, too-soft texture.) Did you know that Brussels sprouts are a great source of vitamins C and K? Well, now you do.

Butternut Squash

65 calories and 3 grams of fiber per cup

This winter squash resembles an oversized pear with a cream-colored exterior. It's mostly solid with a bulbous end that contains seeds and strings to be scooped out. It's full of fiber and vitamins, and it even contains some omega-3 fatty acids. B-nut squash tastes a lot like sweet potato, but it's lighter and lower in starchy carbs; it has around half the calories of sweet potato. Use it to make stews, casseroles, home fries and, our favorite, FRENCH FRIES! Ultimately, it can go anywhere potatoes are normally used. Just peel off that tough skin, discard the stringy insides, and then slice, cube, or shred to your heart's content!

Veggies to Bake Into Fries!

Turn your oven to 425 degrees, and cut the veggies below into French-fry-shaped spears. Line 'em up on a baking sheet (or two) sprayed with nonstick spray, and sprinkle with salt. Bake for 30 to 40 minutes (depending on the thickness of your spears), flipping halfway through cooking, and voilà! Here's how each measures up . . .

Butternut squash. Our go-to for baked fries. However, prepping them DOES take some effort and time—you need to peel them as well as remove all the seeds and stringy fibers. This is the only downside.

Kabocha squash. Since kabocha skin is reasonably thin, you can get away with not peeling it, which ROCKS. The taste? SO GOOD! The trouble slicing it and scooping out the insides? It's there, but it's worth it.

Carrots. These are a LOT easier to prep than the squash options. Not super-crispy, but they taste AMAZING!

Turnips. Slightly cabbage-y in taste, but still a VERY respectable French-fry swap.

Sweet potatoes/yams. Fries made from these are tasty and great if you're in the mood for something starchy. But the calories add up fast!

Russet potatoes. There's a reason potato fries are so popular. They're fantastic. Like sweet potatoes and yams, the calories add up quickly. But if you crave real potato fries, bake 'em at home instead of ordering at the diner or drive-thru.

Cabbage
20 calories and 1.5 grams of fiber per cup

Looking for a happy medium between lettuce wraps and tortillas? Try steaming or boiling green cabbage leaves. You don't need a full-on recipe for stuffed cabbage (although a great one can be found at **hungry-girl.com**); just add your ingredients of choice and wrap 'em up! Chopped veggie-burger patties with pickles and condiments? Sure! Lean ground turkey cooked up with crushed tomatoes? Why not? Cabbage also tastes great sautéed with a bit of light butter, salt, and black pepper. Serve it as a side dish or mix it in with stir-frys.

See also . . . Cole slaw mix, in the Best Bagged Produce section!

Carrots: Whole and Baby

25 calories and 2 grams of fiber per medium-sized carrot or for 8 baby carrots

Whole carrots are great for stews and soups, but baby carrots are fantastic popped straight into your mouth or with a little dip. These are a great fridge staple for mindless munchers . . . A crunchy fix for not a lot of calories. Sweet! FYI, carrots dipped in salsa = AWESOME. Not crazy about raw carrots? Roast 'em! You can mix up a simple sweet glaze from low-sugar or sugar-free apricot preserves, light butter, and spices to serve on your roasted carrots; or let your carrots cook all day with that glaze in a crock pot 'til they're nice and tender.

Cauliflower

25 calories and 2 grams of fiber per cup

Much like broccoli, cauliflower's great both as a snack and as a recipe ingredient. Try it in casseroles and even blended into soup as a creamy, fiber-packed thickener! When steamed until soft and mashed, cauliflower blends seamlessly into mashed potatoes. You can even use it as a full-on swap! Just add a little light butter, fat-free creamer, and plenty of seasonings. It's also amazing at filling out potato salads—boil or steam it just slightly, and it works perfectly.

Celery

6 calories and 0.5 grams of fiber per stalk or for 10 sticks

Like baby carrots, celery sticks are perfect for chomping on between meals. They're a little bland on their own, so they're best with flavorful dips: Fiery salsa, creamy Dijon mustard, and light blue cheese dressing all work well! Other good uses? Chop it up and add to soups and stir-frys for bulk—it tastes great lightly cooked, and adding celery to already-flavorful dishes is a good way to keep it from being boring.

Cucumbers

16 calories and 0.5 grams of fiber per cup

From oversized options to the short and slim, cucumbers are super-delicious. Slice 'em up and add to salads and sandwiches. Make your sandwich seem even larger by serving it open-faced and piling it high with crispy green cucumber slices. A fun mini recipe? Thinly slice several seedless (or seeded) cucumbers and cover in seasoned rice vinegar. The result is crunchy, slightly sweet sunomono salad (a Japanese dish) that you can snack on all day long. Add crab or shrimp to the salad for a low-calorie protein fix. Another idea? Add chopped cucumber to fruit salad to get more bang for your calorie buck. The juice from citrus fruits and berries will seep into the cucumbers, and you won't even know the chopped cukes are there! They'll blend right in with the sweet stuff.

Eggplant
20 calories and 3 grams of fiber per cup

In addition to being beauteous (it's PURPLE!), eggplant is delicious whether cooked in a skillet or baked in the oven. Enjoy it hot in Italian dishes, or chill it and add to salads. For a fun appetizer, serve it chilled and topped with basil, tomato, and a drizzle of balsamic vinegar. So good! Use eggplant slices as alternate layers with the noodles in lasagna—you'll save a ton of carby calories, and it tastes amazing!

HG's TOP ATE
"Put It On The Grill" Fruits & Veggies!

Why should meat have all the fun at a BBQ? Try these at your next cookout . . . or just on a grill pan indoors.

1. **Bell peppers.** Cut one in half, pull out the seeds, and grill; then fill it with some guilt-free scoopable salad, or slice it up for a sandwich topping or veggie side dish!

2. **Portabella mushroom caps.** A super-simple swap for burgers and veggie patties alike.

3. **Eggplant.** Slice into slabs and lay 'em on the grill; they make a great filling for wraps!

4. **Zucchini.** Sliced and grilled zucchini is a super side dish, and it tastes great in a wrap with that eggplant!

5. **Pineapple rings.** SO GOOD, fresh or canned! Let 'em caramelize on both sides (a little nonstick spray on the grill is all it takes), and then slap one on a burger or serve with a sweet dip made from light yogurt, vanilla extract, and sweetener.

6. **Mango.** How do you make mango slices even better? Sprinkle 'em with some cayenne pepper, grill, and serve with grilled chicken breast!

7. **Butternut squash.** Cut it into cubes and grill it on a stick, kebab-style! Pssst . . . those cubes taste awesome dipped in ketchup.

8. **Onion.** Grill sliced or quartered onions until softened and slightly blackened, and you've got a delicious addition to sandwiches, wraps, and more!

Jicama
25 calories and 3 grams of fiber per ½ cup

If you've never experienced the sheer joy of jicama, head to the market NOW. It looks sort of like a huge radish in a shade of pale yellow. But it has a mild sweetness and the texture of an apple. Crisp, refreshing, crunchy, awesome! Slice it up and chomp away, or cut it into matchstick-sized strips and add to salads. Just make sure you peel it first . . .

Kabocha Squash
65 calories and 3 grams of fiber per cup

This Japanese pumpkin isn't a staple in every supermarket, but it's definitely worth seeking out. Just look for a small, speckled, green pumpkin; or ask a friendly stock boy. Similar to butternut squash (only less watery and with a little more "personality"), it's sweet and works perfectly well as a potato swap. You can also use kabocha in pretty much any recipe that calls for butternut squash—HELLO, baked kabocha fries! P.S. The skin is totally edible and fairly tender so you don't have to peel it first if you don't want to.

Kale
35 calories and 1.5 grams of fiber per cup

An amazing find in the produce aisle! The dark-colored leaves taste good (though slightly bitter) when steamed, baked, or stir-fried. It's also known among nutrition professionals as one of the healthiest veggies around. When spritzed with nonstick spray, sprinkled with salt, and baked at a high temperature until crispy, kale takes on a potato-chip-like texture and taste. And since you can eat a huge amount for very few calories, it's an ideal snack for cravers of crunchy, salty things.

Lettuce: Romaine, Iceberg, Butter, and Field Greens
8 calories and 1 gram of fiber per cup

Everyone has their favorites, and in HG Land it's all about the romaine. The leafy green is beyond perfect for chopped salads, sandwich topping, and lettuce wraps. Heads of iceberg are fun for creating retro wedge salads, and shredded iceberg is your best bet for Mexican tacos, burritos, fajitas, and more—the crisp pieces match really well with creamy 'n cool sour cream (fat-free, of course) and zesty salsa. Use butter lettuce (a.k.a. Bibb) as tasty lettuce cups, and fill them with delicious guilt-free items. Field greens will make your homemade salads feel as fancy as restaurant versions.

See also . . . the Best Bagged Produce section!

PRODUCE

Mushrooms: White and Brown (Especially Portabella)
20 calories and 1 gram of fiber per cup or per portabella mushroom

Raw mushrooms are best sliced and added to salads. But for the most part, these veggies are even better when cooked. Sliced mushrooms work really well as a topping for pizza-ish recipes— anything featuring pizza sauce and part-skim mozzarella. They're also fantastic in egg dishes—scrambles, omelettes, frittatas, and b-fast casseroles. And they're delicious cooked into chili and other tomato-based dishes. Add chopped brown mushrooms to anything with ground meat; you'll get meaty flavor and texture without a lot of extra calories. Stir-fry some portabella strips for a steak-like addition to fajitas, stir-frys, salads, and more. You can even swap out meat entirely for portabella mushrooms. Use the oversized cap as a burger swap.

Onions: White, Yellow, and Red
55 calories and 2 grams of fiber per cup

White, yellow, and red onions are ideal for skillet meals, egg dishes, and Italian-style items. White onions are your basic blank canvas, yellow onions have a sweet flavor when cooked for a long time, and red onions have bite. One of the best ways to enjoy an onion? Slice it into rings and faux-fry it! **(See page 24 for the 411 on faux-frying.)**

Fast-Fix Alert! Wanna quickly infuse your food with flavor? Pop over to the spices section of the supermarket and grab some dried minced onion.

Potato Warning! Weigh Your Spuds . . .

Sweet potatoes, yams, basic baking potatoes . . . The stats aren't too bad, with about 20 to 30 calories per ounce. But it is EXTREMELY important to weigh them if you're counting calories. Most people assume the average potato weighs in at about 6 ounces (around 150 calories). At the HG HQ, we've found that the standard spud tips the scales at 12 ounces (more like 300 calories)—no exaggeration! We prefer our potato swaps anyway, like butternut squash and mashed cauliflower . . . And this is part of the reason why.

Scallions (a.k.a. Green Onions)
35 calories and 2.5 grams of fiber per cup

A topping of raw scallions adds a little crunch and flavor to salads and anything Mexican-inspired, from quesadillas to nachos. Cooked scallions work well in Chinese-inspired dishes too. Got leftover scallions? Chop them up for a tasty and simple garnish on your dinner. Schmancy!

Snow Peas and Sugar Snap Peas
15 calories and 1 gram of fiber for 10 pods

Sweet, crisp, and ultimately awesome. These peapods are an ideal snack option. (**Check out our TOP ATE Veggies for Snacking On Raw list on page 64!**) Also a great way to add crunch to salad, and they're amazing lightly steamed and tossed with low-fat sesame ginger dressing. Yum! It's another veggie that's perfect for stir-frys; no chopping required.

Spaghetti Squash
30 calories and 2 grams of fiber per cup

Enjoy it alone or use it to supersize your pasta! Here's how to make it: Cut one in half and remove the seeds; then microwave (in a covered dish with ¼ cup water) or bake until tender. Use a fork to scrape out the spaghetti squash strands, and you're done! Toss 1½ cups squash with a serving of whole-wheat spaghetti. You'll DOUBLE your pasta's portion size!

HG Trick! No need to trash the seeds from your winter squashes. When roasted in the oven, they turn into a great snack—a quarter-cup serving of roasted seeds has about 70 calories and 3 grams of fat.

Spinach
7 calories and 0.5 grams of fiber per cup

Spinach works as a salad base and is fantastic cooked in stir-frys and steamed dishes. It cooks super-quickly (so don't leave it unattended in a skillet!), making it great in scrambles and egg mugs. (**Check out page 205 for more egg essentials.**) The pre-chopped frozen kind is ideal in recipes, but opt for fresh leaves if assembling a salad plate or simple stovetop dish.

Tomatoes: Plum, Beefsteak, Cherry, and Grape
20 calories and 1.5 grams of fiber per medium tomato
or for ¾ cup cherry or grape tomatoes

The larger types are perfect for salads, sandwiches, wraps . . . You can even hollow them out, fill 'em with protein like tuna or chicken (and your condiments of choice), and bake until soft. Yum! The smaller varieties are sweet and juicy—perfect for snacking on. And, yes, we know . . . technically, the tomato is a fruit!

See also . . . the Canned Tomatoes section.

Turnips
35 calories and 2.5 grams of fiber per cup

Fans of cabbage and French fries alike will want to give turnips a try. Why? When sliced into spears and baked at a high temperature, turnips become almost crisp like potato fries, just with an ever-so-slight cabbage flavor. Just be sure to scrub your turnips very well or peel them.

Zucchini and Crookneck (a.k.a. Yellow) Squash
35 calories and 2 grams of fiber per squash

Summer squash tastes spectacular, especially grilled until charred or baked until soft. Use it in frittatas, scrambles, salads, and sauced-up veggie side dishes. Slice zucchini into thin ribbons, and steam or boil them until tender. Then toss with fettuccine noodles to bulk up your pasta for hardly any calories.

HG's TOP ATE Veggies for Snacking On Raw

Yes, some of these are technically fruits. But for the purposes of this TOP ATE list, they're veggies all the way . . .

1. Broccoli florets
2. Cherry and grape tomatoes
3. Snow peas and sugar snap peas
4. Red, yellow, and orange bell pepper strips
5. Jicama sticks
6. Baby carrots
7. Cucumber slices
8. Celery strips

Salad Mixes

Pre-chopped lettuce blends with colorful veggie accessories?
Awesome. There are many to choose from. Seek out mixes like
American (iceberg, carrot shreds, and red cabbage), spring mix
(a schmancy assortment of baby lettuces), and Italian (romaine and
radicchio). Fantastic!

Bagged Salad Heads-Up

Beware of bagged kits with dressing packets, dried fruit, and
assorted crunchy toppings. While they're great in theory, they
typically contain 2 to 4 servings, despite the fact that most people
would consider each a single-serving package. Factor in full-fat
dressing and oily extras, and you could easily take in more than
40 fat grams without even realizing it. Avoid these or read the
labels VERY carefully!

SUPERSIZING SUPERSTAR! SWAP 'TIL YOU DROP!

Broccoli Cole Slaw

A beauteous and delicious combo of assorted, pre-washed crunchy veggie shreds—broccoli, carrots, and red cabbage. Some even come in ready-to-steam bags. It's as delicious raw as it is cooked. A cup of it has around 25 calories and 3 grams of fiber. Here are some fun uses to get you started . . .

PRODUCE

* Create a filling, fruity salsa topper for chicken, fish, and more! Just add some shreds to sweet jarred salsa and marinate overnight in the fridge. You'll have a slightly crunchy and completely delicious way to zazzle up any boring protein dish.

* Add steamed slaw to saucy frozen entrées. It's a fantastic way to fill out meals and snacks. Another trick up BCS's sleeve? Use it to fill out deli salads. After some time in the fridge, the shreds will soften and soak up loads of flavor.

* **Hot Couple Alert!** Just add dressing. Toss with low-fat sesame ginger for an amazing Asian slaw. Thai peanut dressing is soooo good with steamed slaw—like a cold sesame noodle swap! Or try some fruity vinaigrette for a sweet slaw. Just make sure you read the dressing labels carefully and stick to low-fat ones with 30 calories or so per tablespoon.

* Broccoli cole slaw is an amazing pasta swap. Just cook the slaw until soft (in the microwave or on the stove), and then add chunky tomato sauce. Instant saucy satisfaction, and you can eat a giant bowl of it for a totally reasonable amount of calories. Success!

* Believe it or not, broc slaw makes an excellent omelette ingredient. And since it already includes a variety of veggies, you really don't need to add anything other than fat-free liquid egg substitute (or egg whites) and maybe a little low-fat cheese. Just cook the shreds in a pan with nonstick spray until softened, and then add your egg swap. Scramble or flip it up omelette-style, and enjoy!

Classic Cole Slaw

While broccoli slaw is more versatile (and delicious), classic slaw mix has its place too. Use it in warm Asian salad, soft tacos, egg rolls, wraps, and veggied-up ground meat! A 2-cup serving of this stuff has just 25 calories or so and 2 grams of fiber.

Bean Sprouts

Like lots of other bagged veggies, these can often be steamed up right in the bag. They're an IDEAL addition to saucy frozen dinners and Chinese takeout. Crunch without the excess calories! A cup contains about 30 calories and 2 grams of fiber.

~ HERBS ~

FIVE FRESH HERBS IN A FLASH

Here's a list of which fresh herbs are worth having on hand and what kinds of dishes they work well in. P.S. They're virtually calorie-free!

Dill — Dips, seafood, and deli-style salads

Basil — Italian and Greek

Mint — Beverages and desserts

Parsley — Italian and Greek

Cilantro — Mexican

~ FROZEN VEGETABLES ~

In addition to the eight great picks above, here are a few frozen vegetable varieties that deserve some special attention . . .

Seasoned Veggies and Veggies in Low-Fat Sauce

What could be easier than pre-spiced and pre-sauced veggie sides? Mostly, you'll find cheese sauces and light butter options. These are usually very reasonable in the fat and calorie departments. (Check the fat content and the servings per bag to be sure.)

HG Standout: Green Giant Just for One!

These single-serving trays are life-changing (assuming that food's an important part of your life). Enjoy one as is for a hot 'n savory snack, or combine it with other items. Try scooping the insides out of that leftover baked potato and filling it with cheesy cauliflower. Or puree the prepped contents of a broccoli and cheese tray with a little plain light soymilk for a creamy broc 'n cheese soup. The Just for One lineup includes several varieties, each with 40 to 80 calories, 1 to 2 grams of fat, and 3 grams of fiber.

Steam-in-the-Bag Veggies

Next to the microwave itself, microwave-ready bags may be the best thing to happen to frozen veggies. Look for mixed produce, solo veggies, and lightly seasoned or sauced varieties. These are pricier than standard bagged veggies, but they are worth it if you're unlikely to cook vegetables otherwise. If you don't mind the extra step, save cash and stick with the regular bags; then see our How to Steam Your Own box below and DIY!

How to Steam Your Own Veggies

You don't need a stovetop steamer. Just put veggies in a microwave-safe bowl with an inch or so of water. Cover the bowl with a microwave-safe top (an upside-down plate works well). Microwave until thawed, 5 minutes or so. Continue to nuke them in one-minute intervals, until your desired texture is achieved. (Less time leads to crisp veggies; more time yields tender veggies.)

~ FRESH FRUIT ~

The ABCs of Fruit!

Next up . . . alphabetical, fruity fun! Scan the list or search for the deets on YOUR favorite items—either way, you're getting informed . . .

Apples: Fuji, Granny Smith, and More
100 calories and 4.5 grams of fiber per medium-sized apple

Fujis are the perfect blend of crisp, sweet, and tart—they work in just about any recipe that calls for apples. Granny Smiths are great when you crave something tart and tangy. In general, apples are amazing, raw or cooked. Raw, they can be enjoyed as snacks and in salads, parfaits, oatmeal, cold cereal, slaws, etc. Cooked, they're ideal in desserts . . . just make sure the other ingredients are light to keep your treat guilt-free.

Avocado

115 calories, 11 grams of fat, and 5 grams of fiber per 2.5 ounces (about ½ cup sliced)

While it is high in fat, it's also super-healthy, and a little goes a long way. Whip up a chunky guilt-free guacamole by mixing a few slices with red onions, cherry tomatoes, lime juice, and some fat-free sour cream or Greek yogurt. (Add mashed peas to bulk up your dip for fewer calories than a whole avocado.) Spread a little on some turkey slices, or dice a few slices and toss onto your salads.

PRODUCE

How Do You Like THEM Apples?

Here are some tips when you go apple picking in the produce aisle . . .

Fuji: An HG staple, it's the best all-around apple. Red skin, often with some yellow; crispy and firm with just a hint of tartness to cut through the natural sweetness. Good as a snack, a recipe ingredient, and more.

Granny Smith: Tart and green. Great for snacking on, but not the best to bake with—we like sweet apple desserts but don't want to add too much extra sugar!

Gala: The skin can be any combination of reds, yellows, and pinks, or it can be plain solid red. The flavor is mild and sweet, and though they're generally firm and crisp, they can turn out grainy. Trivia tidbit! Galas are related to the next apple on the list . . .

Golden Delicious: Large, with yellow skin and sweet-tasting flesh. These apples are yummy BUT they do bruise easily, so be careful. They're good eaten raw or cooked.

Honeycrisp: Similar to Fujis; has red 'n yellow skin, and tastes sweet but not TOO sweet. A fan favorite!

McIntosh: This old-school beauty is red with green flecks on the outside and white on the inside. It's slightly tart, perfect for pies, and is a great snacking apple.

Pink Lady: Pretty blush pink and yellow skin, sweet yet tart in taste, crispy in texture, and especially ideal for raw snacking.

Red Delicious: This variety of apples has become much less popular in recent years; the red skin is tempting, but the flavor is mild and not that interesting. They also often end up with a mealy, unappealing texture and taste.

Rome: Gorgeous glossy red skin BUT this is not the best snacking apple; the flavor develops more once cooked. If you're into baked apples, this is your best bet!

APPLE BFFS!

The Laughing Cow Light Creamy Swiss Cheese Wedges
It might seem like a slightly odd combo, but spread some of this cheese on your apple slices, and you'll be SOLD.

Light or Low-Fat Caramel Apple Dip
This one's kind of a "duh" pairing, but it's too good NOT to mention. Who doesn't dream of slathering chunks of apple with gooey, creamy, dreamy caramel!?!

Reduced-Fat Peanut Butter
A classic duo. Peanut butter is a little fat-and-calorie dense, though, even the reduced-fat kind. But a little can go a LONG way, so don't just go loading your apple slices up with too much nut butter! Smear a tablespoon of the fat-slashed kind over a medium apple's worth of slices, and you've got a deliciously filling super-snack for under 200 calories and about 6 grams of fat. Sweet!

Fat-Free Cottage Cheese or Yogurt
Along with a little vanilla extract, cinnamon, and sweetener, this makes for an amazing no-cook snack or breakfast component. When it comes to yogurt, go for fat-free Greek or bulk up your favorite flavor. **Yoplait Light Apple Turnover**? We're coming for you . . .

Bananas
105 calories and 3 grams of fiber per medium-sized banana

Bananas are filling, good for you, and delicious. And they're real transformers, too. How so? Just slice and freeze them fully. Then pop the pieces in your mouth whole for a sweet snack, toss 'em in a blender for a freezy ice-cream-like fix, or use them in smoothies for fun texture and flavor. Go bananas!

FUN WITH . . . FROZEN BANANAS!

STEP 1: Slice banana into coins.

STEP 2: Place in a plastic bag.

STEP 3: Place bag in the freezer, arranging it so the banana coins are as spread out as possible to avoid freezing together.

Once your banana coins are frozen, they are officially ideal for adding to your smoothies and shakes for extra thickness and creaminess.

HG Snack Idea: Before you freeze the coins, spoon a dollop of Cool Whip Free onto one, then top with another banana coin. Freeze the mini sandwiches for cool 'n tasty bites. And feel free to mix a bit of reduced-fat peanut butter or light chocolate syrup in with the whipped topping first!

Berries: Strawberries, Raspberries, Blackberries, and Blueberries

55 calories and 3.5 grams of fiber per cup of strawberries
65 calories and 8 grams of fiber per cup of raspberries/blackberries
85 calories and 3.5 grams of fiber per cup of blueberries

Summer is berry season! And since these are some of the priciest picks in the off-season, enjoy them on the cheap when you can. They're perfect for parfaits, cereal bowls, baked desserts, and snacking. Toss 'em all together for a fun fruit salad to keep in the fridge—whenever you're craving something sweet, you've got something ready to go.

Berry BFF! It's all about the low-fat dairy. Add berries to yogurt (flavored, Greek, frozen . . . whatever!), cottage cheese, light ice cream, and sugar-free pudding.

Cherries

100 calories and 3 grams of fiber per cup

Sweet cherries are insanely delicious in recipes and as a stand-alone snack. If you do decide to whip up a recipe—like guilt-free baked goodies or a slushy blended fruit drink—definitely go for frozen dark sweet cherries, which come without pits. If you want to top off an ice cream sundae with retro flair, buy bottled maraschinos (8 calories a pop). But for straight snacking or stirring into spoonable treats like yogurt, it's fresh cherries all the way.

Clementines

35 calories and 1.5 grams of fiber per clementine

Clementines are a type of mandarin orange that are sweet, juicy, and seedless. They're easy to peel and less acidic than regular oranges. They're often stocked and sold in crates, and they sometimes go by the name Cuties. Awwwwww! Great for straight-up snacking. You can also peel, chop, and toss 'em into salads, wraps, etc.

Cranberries

45 calories and 4.5 grams of fiber per cup

These red berries are a holiday staple in baked desserts, but they require a warning. Since they're so tart, most people end up adding a LOT of sweetener. To really get at their natural sweetness, cook them for a long time ('til they burst). Then consider using granulated no-calorie sweetener (like Splenda or stevia)—either in place of sugar, or in combination with it.

PRODUCE

Grapefruit
55 calories and 2 grams of fiber per grapefruit

These thick-skinned orbs are packed with vitamins and are a fun change from everyday citrus, but they're a little tart. Try throwing a few segments onto a green salad; the juice acts as dressing . . . Talk about a multi-tasker! Or sprinkle half a grapefruit with a bit of sweetener, broil it, and eat it for dessert (or breakfast . . . whatever!). And if peeling fresh grapefruit stresses you out (so much thick skin!), buy the segments packaged in natural juice.

Grapes: Green and Red
100 calories and 1 gram of fiber per cup

Grapes are great. Eat them as is or freeze them for a sweet 'n icy snack. And don't be afraid to use them in savory dishes, like chunky chicken salad and fruity salsa. Need another reason to eat grapes? They're good for your heart. Sweet!

Mangos
135 calories and 4 grams of fiber per mango

When it comes to sweet, tropical, juicy fruits, mango is one of our top picks. In addition to being insanely delicious, it's also loaded with vitamin C, fiber, and antioxidants. Good in salads, parfaits, savory dishes, sweet items . . . or just eaten plain!

Melon: Watermelon, Cantaloupe, and Honeydew
45 calories and 1 gram of fiber per cup of watermelon

60 calories and 1.5 grams of fiber per cup of cantaloupe or honeydew melon

If you like your fruit large, juicy, and sweet, melons are your friends. Crack one open (not literally; use a knife), and dive right in. Toss chunks with berries and citrus segments, or enjoy 'em solo.

Nectarines
60 calories and 2.5 grams of fiber per nectarine

Nectarines are the smooth, fuzz-free cousins of peaches. When good and ripe, nectarines are incredibly juicy (read: messy), so they're not your best bet if you're on the go. But their sweetness makes them a great ingredient for desserts and blended drinks—less need for added sweetener!

PRODUCE

Oranges
75 calories and 3.5 grams of fiber per orange

Do yourself a favor . . . Next time you're considering chugging orange juice, reach for one of these instead. The actual fruit is far more filling and satisfying—and a better calorie bargain as well. As for that OJ? Stick to light juice drinks. (See the Beverages section for the 411!)

Peaches
60 calories and 2 grams of fiber per peach

This multi-purpose fruit can be found all over the market; buy it fresh, sliced and frozen, or sliced and packed in juice. Fresh peaches are great for snacking on, but only if they're ripe and juicy. Frozen peach slices can actually be thawed and enjoyed the same as fresh, so thaw a few slices and add to fruit salads and breakfast bowls. For recipes and snack assembly requiring super-juicy slices, opt for the canned or jarred kind packed in juice.

HG's TOP ATE
Types of Fruit to Add to Salsa

Whether it's salsa from scratch or store-bought stuff that you punch up with fruit, these are the best picks . . .

1. Mango
2. Peaches
3. Grapes
4. Plums
5. Strawberries
6. Pineapple
7. Avocado
8. Blueberries

HG FYI: Finely chop the majority of these; halve or quarter the grapes, and keep the blueberries whole!

Pears
95 calories and 5 grams of fiber per pear

An often-overlooked grab-n-go option. Some people like them firm and crunchy; others enjoy them soft and sweet. Either way, pears are a tasty alternative to apples. BUT be careful—pears bruise easily, so you might want to protect them and not just toss one into your bag while running out the door.

HG's TOP ATE
Unconventional Fruits & Veggies for Your Salad

If you haven't before, give these toppers a try!

1. Corn. Whether you start with canned niblets or frozen kernels, corn is a great salad topping. If you go canned, rinse the corn before you top your greens to cut back on salt; if you use the frozen stuff, cook it briefly in a skillet until lightly blackened. Good stuff!

2. Mandarin orange segments. Not only are these fun to add to your greens, but also the juice acts as a bit of a dressing booster. Great with broccoli slaw, chopped chicken, and low-fat sesame ginger dressing.

3. Pears and apples. These are both good sliced and added to salads that include salty cheeses, like fat-free or reduced-fat feta!

4. Hearts of palm. Ever wonder, "What in the WORLD are hearts of palm?" They're veggies harvested from certain palm tree buds, and they taste great on top of a salad.

5. Beets. Don't be scared of beets. Sure, they're aggressively fuschia and will stain everything if you aren't careful, but they're SO good chopped and added to salads. And yes, they will tinge your salad with a magenta hue, but that's part of the fun.

6. Jicama. You really should give this stuff a try. Chop it and toss it into your salad . . . It goes well with pretty much anything you might have in there!

7. Strawberries. Think about how much you like strawberries. Now think about how much more fun eating a salad would be if it had sliced strawberries. See?

8. Sun-dried tomatoes. So much flavor packed into each shriveled tomato! Look for pouches to avoid the oil these are commonly packed in, or just pat away most of the oil before topping your greens.

Plums
30 calories and 1 gram of fiber per plum

Plums taste great, and THREE of them clock in at under 100 calories. Not bad! The purple-skinned fruits are often sweeter, while the ruby reds are more tart. Make a fun and fruity salsa by adding diced plum to standard tomato salsa or toss some plum slices into a salad. Mmmmm . . .

PRODUCE

No-Sugar-Added Frozen Fruit:
Strawberries, Dark Sweet Cherries, Mango Chunks, Peach Slices, and Mixed Berries

Unsweetened frozen fruit is perfect for smoothies (with some light yogurt and light soymilk), slushies (with crushed ice and light juice drinks), and guilt-free blended cocktails. It's also great to snack on straight—just let it thaw a little first.

HG Heads-Up
It's not important that the "No Sugar Added" claim be splashed all over the front of the package; more often than not, it won't be. What's important is that you flip over that bag and eye the ingredients list. It should be just fruit; nothing added. Syrup, fructose, cane juice, and good old-fashioned sugar can double the calorie count. Not necessary!

" HG! When should I use frozen fruit instead of fresh fruit? "

It's kind of on a case-by-case basis. Smoothies are an obvious answer, but frozen fruit can be used for SO much more . . .

Frozen strawberries are great for making a sweet, fruity sauce for desserts, waffles, and pancakes. Just microwave them until thawed and soft; they'll release some juice. Then mash 'em with a fork, mix with some low-sugar or sugar-free strawberry preserves, and you're set.

Frozen peach slices are easy to blend into a sorbet-like treat; just add a splash of your favorite low-calorie, fruit-flavored beverage, blend 'til smooth, and spoon! They're also useful when making fruity baked desserts. Why? No pitting, no peeling. Nice . . .

Frozen dark sweet cherries get instant points for having no pits. And they taste AMAZING layered with sugar-free chocolate pudding or stirred into light vanilla yogurt.

Frozen mango chunks are very similar to ordinary ripe mango once defrosted. And since separating mango from its core is a bit of a chore, use frozen mango anytime you don't feel like cutting up a fresh one.

BUDGET-FRIENDLY PRODUCE GUIDE:
SEASONAL SAVINGS!

You can save a lot of cash by buying produce when it's in season; as an added bonus, that's when it tastes the best!

Year-Round Favorites

Bell Peppers
Onions
Scallions
Broccoli
Cauliflower
Cabbage
Carrots
Celery
Mushrooms
Snow Peas and Sugar Snap
  Peas
Lettuce & Spinach
Jicama
Tomatoes
Avocado
Apples
Bananas

Springtime Fruits & Veggies

Artichokes
Mango
Asparagus

Summer

Berries
Grapes
Zucchini and Crookneck
  Squash
Cherries
Nectarines
Peaches
Plums
Cucumbers
Melon
Eggplant

Wintertime Produce Picks

Butternut Squash
Kabocha Squash
Spaghetti Squash
Kale
Oranges
Brussels Sprouts
Clementines
Grapefruit

Fall for Autumn Fruits & Veggies

Pears
Turnips
Cranberries

PRODUCE

CANNED FOODS

~ CANNED FRUIT ~

The 411 on Canned Fruit: Juice vs. Syrups, Etc.

Wondering about the differences between fruit packed in water, juice, light syrup, and heavy syrup? Here's how they measure up, on average . . .

½ cup fruit packed in water =
30 to 45 calories, 7 to 12g carbs, 7 to 10g sugars

½ cup fruit packed in juice =
45 to 70 calories, 12 to 18g carbs, 10 to 16g sugars

½ cup fruit packed in light syrup =
70 to 80 calories, 17 to 20g carbs, 16 to 20g sugars

½ cup fruit packed in heavy syrup =
90 to 110 calories, 22 to 28g carbs, 19 to 28g sugars

What's Up with Water-Packed Fruit?

Artificial sweetener is often added to cans of fruit packed in water, so keep that in mind and check labels if you prefer to avoid it. But fruit packed in water has the least amount of sugar, which makes it ideal for those watching their sugar intake. Look for labels that include the words "No Sugar Added" to be sure.

Bottom Line: We prefer juice-packed fruit, since it has plenty of natural sweetness without packing in too many calories or too much excess sugar.

Pineapple Packed in Juice:
Crushed, Tidbits, Chunks, and Slices/Rings

Each of these shapes and sizes has its time and place. Use crushed pineapple to infuse juicy goodness and pulpy texture into desserts, pancake batter, and drinks, from smoothies to cocktails! Tidbits are terrific when you want actual fruit bits that go a long way; use these in salads and slaws. When you want to chomp into sizable fruit pieces, opt for chunks—they're amazing on skewers and in sweet Asian dishes. And use the slices/rings for layering up everything from sandwiches and burgers to cakes and trifles. A ½-cup serving, or 3 rings, has around 70 calories and 1 gram of fiber.

Mandarin Oranges Packed in Juice

Mmmm, sweet little segments of citrus. Perfect for Chinese chicken salad, teriyaki stir-frys . . . even fruity relish or a fun spin on salsa. Half of a cup has about 45 calories and 1 gram of fiber.

HG Snack Idea: Drain and mix some with sugar-free vanilla pudding for a Creamsicle-inspired treat!

Peach Slices Packed in Juice

Need guaranteed-to-be-sweet-and-juicy peaches? These ROCK. They're a great staple to keep around when making parfaits, oatmeal, and dessert-inspired snacks. A ½ cup has about 55 calories and 1.5 grams of fiber. For smoothies, though, opt for frozen slices.

HG Snack Idea: Top with cinnamon, crushed graham crackers, and a scoop of light vanilla ice cream to quickly feed a craving for cobbler à la mode!

To Drain or Not to Drain?

Keep the juice when a little liquid and added sweetness will help, not hinder, a dish—beverages and saucy dishes are top candidates for undrained fruit. Lightly drain your fruit when the extra liquid would throw off the texture or when you want the occasional POP of fruity flavor as opposed to overall sweetness.

No-Sugar-Added Applesauce

This is usually jarred or packed in individual containers. A ½-cup serving contains around 50 calories and 2 grams of fiber. Not bad! Applesauce is great for baking—it'll keep your food moist without the need for butter, eggs, and oil. Add a little cinnamon or pumpkin pie spice for a sweet spoonable treat. Or look for flavored varieties—these are most often available in the single-serving cups. The individual cups are a fantastic snack to stash anywhere resources—like can openers, measuring cups, and refrigerators—are limited.

HG HOT COUPLE!

No-Sugar-Added Applesauce + Cake Mix

PER SERVING (¹⁄₁₂ᵗʰ of cake, 1 piece): 180 calories, 3g fat, 299mg sodium, 36g carbs, 0.5g fiber, 21.5g sugars, 1.5g protein

Mix a cup of the fruit sauce with an 18.25-ounce box of moist-style cake mix. Add 1 cup of water and whisk until smooth. Transfer to a baking pan sprayed with nonstick spray, and bake in the oven until a knife inserted into the center comes out clean. (Refer to cake-mix box for pan size and approximate bake time.) You've just made a moist and fluffy cake with way fewer calories and fat grams than standard cake!

Pure Pumpkin

Canned pumpkin is essentially cooked and pureed pumpkin. Keep cans of it in the pantry at all times, as it's an HG staple. Pumpkin is super-low in calories (40 per ½-cup serving), has practically no fat, and is loaded with fiber (about 4 grams per serving). Pumpkin ROCKS. If you can't find this in the regular canned foods aisle, look for it in the baking aisle.

HG Standout: Libby's. The consistency is perfectly smooth and creamy. The flavor is right on—slightly sweet and completely delicious. And it's a gorgeous shade of bright orange.

HG Heads-Up
Don't confuse canned pure pumpkin (the good stuff) with pumpkin pie filling (which is loaded with sugar). Pumpkin pie filling has more than THREE times as many calories!

HG's TOP ATE Uses for Canned Pure Pumpkin

1. For making two-ingredient brownies. See the HOT COUPLE below!

2. As an oatmeal bowl filler-upper (and fiber-upper)!

3. Mixed with light vanilla yogurt or pudding for a sweet treat!

4. In pancakes, pies, and dessert-inspired dips.

5. For thickening up chili, stew, and creamy soups.

6. In baked goods like muffins and breads as a swap for eggs and oil.

7. Mixed with cumin and other savory seasonings for a super-low-cal refried beans swap!

8. In shakes and smoothies for seasonal flair.

HG HOT COUPLE!

Canned Pure Pumpkin + Devil's Food Cake Mix

PER SERVING ($^1/_{12}$th of recipe, 1 muffin): 181 calories, 3.5g fat, 357mg sodium, 37g carbs, 2g fiber, 20g sugars, 2g protein

Grab a large bowl and combine a 15-ounce can of pumpkin with an 18.25-ounce box of devil's food cake mix. Don't add ANYTHING else. Stir until smooth and fully mixed. Evenly distribute the thick batter into a 12-cup muffin pan sprayed with nonstick spray. Bake at 400 degrees for 20 minutes. Then enjoy!

Unexpected Find:
Pureed Fruit in the Baby Foods Aisle

Applesauce is fantastic, so why not look for other fruit purees? They're hiding in the baby foods aisle. Peaches, bananas, and pears are all sweet and delicious when pureed—not to mention, incredibly healthful and all natural. Use these any place you'd use applesauce, from baking to snacking! These range from 50 to 100 calories and 1 to 3 grams of fiber per 4-ounce jar. Pureed bananas have the most calories, while pear puree contains the most fiber.

Crushed Tomatoes

Canned crushed tomatoes are a GREAT swap or start for marinara sauce, which can be pricey and even high in fat and calories. Half a cup of crushed tomatoes has about 40 calories and 2 grams of fiber. Don't mistake these for diced tomatoes—crushed tomatoes are the fully squashed, practically pureed version of the red fruit. (Yep, tomatoes are technically fruits, not veggies!) There are options on shelves that are seasoned with Italian spices, but you can always buy them plain and flavor 'em up on your own. Crushed tomatoes are less intense than canned tomato sauce and have a fresher taste, so use 'em in recipes when you don't want to add too much salty flavor or concentrated sweetness.

Tomato Sauce

Well, we just told you to use canned crushed tomatoes as red sauce and in certain recipes, so why is standard tomato sauce still on the list? Because it's a great base for low-calorie, flavorful sweet sauces like barbecue, Asian-inspired, and sloppy joe. It's also an amazing ingredient when you want to infuse a lot of flavor without adding much liquid. Half a cup has about 40 calories and 1 gram of fiber.

Fun Fact! While some canned fruits and veggies lose nutrients during the preservation process, tomatoes do not. It's one of the reasons we love them so much!

Tomato Paste

This is the fully concentrated tomato product that is perfect for recipes that require as little extra liquid as possible. Use it to thicken up homemade chili and stew. Add it to meaty sauces that need extra flavor and thickening. Include it in fillings for stuffed veggies and more. A 2-tablespoon serving has about 30 calories and 1 gram of fiber.

HG Tip: It's not just in cans. Look for tomato paste in tubes—it's super-convenient!

Diced Tomatoes

SO many varieties! With onions and garlic? Yup. With Italian herbs and spices? Yup. With green chiles? Totally. Fire-roasted? Absolutely. Fire-roasted tomatoes work especially well as a salsa swap, and they're among the most fresh-tasting items in the canned foods aisle. (Sorry, fruit cocktail.) Depending on the spice profile, this item works with any type of cuisine: Greek, Italian, Mexican, etc. Use these for pitas, wraps, pizzas, omelettes, skillet dishes, soups, and stews. Just about 35 calories, as well as 1.5 grams of fiber, per ½-cup serving.

> **Salt-Slashing 411:** If you love salsa but not the salt content, stock up on cans of salt-free diced tomatoes. Then toss some with your salsa of choice, and the sodium count will come down considerably. Try this trick with other tomato-based sauces and dishes too.

Stewed Tomatoes

Get the "I cooked my tomatoes all day long" taste without the time commitment. Drained or not, a can is super-helpful when you're whipping up no-hassle soups and stews. Making chili? Keep cans of stewed tomatoes with Mexican spices on hand! Want to bulk up store-bought chili? Add the whole can! Each ½ cup has about 35 calories and 2 grams of fiber; a 14.5-ounce can contains about 115 calories and 6.5 grams of fiber.

> **HG Tip:** Sometimes the pieces are pretty large, so you may want to give 'em a rough chop.

Sun-Dried Tomatoes Packed in Oil

Sure they're packed in oil, but they're also packed *with* flavor, which means you don't need a lot of these sweet, shriveled tomatoes to infuse your food of choice with deliciousness. Plus, it's not like you're going to be ingesting all of the oil. Just pluck out the tomatoes and rinse or blot away the excess liquid with paper towels. Not only will this decrease the fat content of your food, but it also keeps the dish from getting overly greasy. A 2-tablespoon serving contains about 30 calories and 3 grams of fat. Try finely chopping and adding them to creamy condiments—like fat-free mayo and The Laughing Cow Light cheese wedges—for crazy-flavorful dips and spreads. Roughly cut them up and add to items like low-fat tuna salad, omelettes, scrambles, and giant leafy-green salads.

> **HG Standout:** Pouched sun-dried tomatoes.
> A great way to avoid that oil altogether!

~ CANNED VEGETABLES ~

(SWAP ALERT!) Sweet Peas

Peas are great in general, but there's one very specific use for them as well. AN HG GUACAMOLE SWAP! The thin skin and soft interior of sweet peas help them to mash up easily and taste creamy. Those labeled "early" or "young" are the best. So mash or puree them and mix with a small amount of avocado for a fat-and-calorie-slashed guac! Season to taste with spices and a splash of lime juice, and stir in chopped tomatoes and veggies to add bulk but not a lot of calories. The peas themselves pack in 60 calories or so and about 3.5 grams of fiber per ½-cup serving.

Sweet Corn Kernels

Another item that's ideal for Mexican-inspired food items—chili and tamale-style dishes are just better with a hint of sweetness, and the canned stuff is easy to work with. Use a few spoonfuls to give a flavor burst to your leafy greens. A ½-cup serving has about 70 calories, 1 gram of fat, and 2 grams of fiber. For sweet corn with less sodium, swing by the frozen foods aisle.

> **HG Standout:** Look for Green Giant Mexicorn, which comes with bits of red and green peppers mixed in!

Jarred Roasted Red Peppers

This is a great ingredient to keep around. The sweet and soft bell peppers are almost always packed in water and are very low in calories. Not only are they terrific in basic salads and sandwich wraps, but they're also an amazing addition to scoopable salads and layered dips. Or puree them and add to sauces and dressings. A 1-ounce piece, about 2 tablespoons once chopped, has around 10 calories.

HG Snack Idea: Top a guilt-free burger patty with a big piece and sprinkle with fat-free or reduced-fat feta for an easy treat with Mediterranean flair.

Jarred Sliced Jalapeño Peppers

These spicy sliced green chiles are a staple for lovers of no-guilt Mexican goodies (tacos, tostadas, nachos—the works!) and spicy foods enthusiasts in general. Use the heat-packed rings to top sandwiches, burgers, and pizza, or chop up a few and stir them into dips and anything else you feel could use some extra spice. Have 2 tablespoons for just 5 calories or so.

HG Alternative! If you like things on the mild side, choose banana pepper slices instead.

Sliced Beets

Beets are sweet and delicious. (It doesn't hurt that they're also beautiful.) These are a fantastic addition to salads, from leafy green ones to scoopable salads like chunky veggies and beans in fruity vinaigrette. Half a cup has just 35 calories or so and 2 grams of fiber. Sometimes they include sugar or salt, but it's usually a minimal amount.

Artichoke Hearts and Bottoms

These are great for adding tangy flavor for very few calories. Blend up with garbanzo beans, broth, and seasonings for a lower-calorie hummus. Pair them with light cheeses (fat-free cream cheese and reduced-fat Parm) and condiments (fat-free mayo and fat-free sour cream) to whip up a slimmed-down spinach-artichoke dip. Or just add them to salads, slaws, and wraps. YUM! A ½ cup has around 35 calories and 2 grams of fiber.

Sliced Black Olives

If you love olives, canned ones are a great pantry staple. The pre-sliced factor will keep you from inhaling them whole by the handful—a good thing, since the fat count adds up fast that way. A 2-tablespoon serving has about 25 calories and 2 grams of fat. These are perfect for topping guilt-free pizzas (or pizza-inspired foods), and Mexican goodies (like nachos and taco salads).

Pickles: Whole, Spears, Chips, and Slices

Pickles are magical. (It's true!) Okay, not in the Harry Potter sense, but they are amazingly tasty on their own and with other items. Use them to top burgers, sandwiches, and anything you want to lend a deli-style or fast-food vibe to. Pickles give you lots of bang for your calorie buck, with about 5 calories per ounce for most (that's about half a pickle). Bread and butter pickles are sweet and higher in calories, with about 20 calories per ounce.

HG Snack Idea: Wrap lean turkey slices around pickles for a salty, protein-packed treat. This is an HG favorite!

HG FYI:
The refrigerated types tend to be more crisp and crunchier, while the shelf-stable varieties are often lower in price.

Pickle Relatives: Relish & Sauerkraut

Use relish to infuse bits of pickle-like goodness into dishes for about 5 to 20 calories per tablespoon. Sauerkraut is basically pickled, shredded cabbage, and it's practically calorie-free. It makes a yummy addition to salads and sandwiches. Use both of these options as hot dog toppers!

Hearts of Palm

These are a fantastic low-calorie salad accessory! They bring a bit of crunch and unique flavor to an otherwise basic bed of greens. They're less intense than artichokes, but they have a similar flavorful bite to them. A ½-cup serving has around 40 calories and 3 grams of fiber.

Where Are All the Other Canned Veggies?

If you're wondering why this section isn't bursting with green beans, spinach, and assorted mixed veggies, it's because the frozen kinds are practically as convenient but much better all around. The frozen versions tend to maintain more of their nutrients, since they're typically flash-frozen at peak ripeness, which locks in vitamins and minerals. The taste and texture are also captured better this way. And canned veggies often contain way more added salt than frozen ones. So flip to **page 68** for more cash-and-time-saving alternatives to fresh vegetables.

The Sodium Situation with Canned Veggies

These are often high in sodium, but several brands make no-salt-added versions. If salt-free is too extreme for your taste buds, try the 50-percent-less-sodium versions. And (fun tip!) rinsing your veggies before eating will eliminate about 20 percent of the sodium content.

Canned Goods in the Latin Foods Aisle

Cans of chipotle peppers in adobo sauce and mild green chiles are good items to keep on hand, in case you need to punch up an otherwise boring food item. Careful, though: That adobo sauce is hot, Hot, HOT!

Canned Goods in the Asian Foods Aisle

Add crunch with bamboo shoots and water chestnuts, and seek out juicy straw mushrooms for that classic Chinese takeout taste! All three options are CRAZY-low in calories.

~ SOUP ~

The average soup serving size is 1 cup, and a 1-cup serving of canned soup weighs in at about 8.5 ounces. So those 14.5-ounce and 15-ounce cans have close to 1¾ cups each. There are larger cans—18 to 19 ounces—that list "about 2 servings" too. Those typically contain just barely more than two 1-cup servings. If you really want to be exact about it, divide the total weight in grams (typically on the front of the can) by the grams per serving (usually in parentheses after the serving size on the nutritional panel)—then multiply all the stats accordingly.

Bottom Line: To make things easy when estimating your intake if you're likely to consume a whole can, just double the per-serving stats. Simple and effective.

Low-Calorie Soup

Think outside the box, er, can, when looking for low-calorie soups. You might see a tempting variety and find it's fairly low in calories, even if it doesn't promote itself as being "light." But when you check the stats, consider the amount you're likely to eat at once; if it's the whole standard-sized can as opposed to a single cup, double those calorie and fat counts.

HG Standouts: Amy's Organic, Amy's Organic Light in Sodium, and Progresso 99% Fat Free, Light, and High Fiber soups.

Freezer-Aisle Finds! Look for heat 'n eat options in the frozen foods section. These are almost always single-serving bowls and cups, which makes checking out the stats a breeze. Tabatchnick is a top brand found at many, many markets.

Microwave-Ready Containers! Tons of brands make ready-to-heat cups, and these are perfect for workplaces, dorm rooms, and anywhere else with a microwave.

Low-Fat Creamy Tomato Soup

The best kinds are slightly sweet with tender chunks of tomato. This pick is insanely versatile. Use it as a swap for tomato sauce. Pour it over chicken and veggies. Or just heat and eat! On average, a cup contains 120 calories, 3 grams of fat, and 2 grams of fiber.

HG All-Star!

Amy's Organic Chunky Tomato Bisque! While it's half a gram too high to qualify for low-fat status (a cup has 130 calories and 3.5 grams of fat), it's undoubtedly our favorite creamy tomato soup. It's exploding with fresh tomato goodness. It's all natural and INCREDIBLE tasting! And there's a Light in Sodium version with half the salt.

BFF: Broccoli cole slaw. This might seem like a strange combo. It's not. Slowly stir-fry the slaw with some soup, so the soup coats the veggies like a sauce. Then cook until the broccoli shreds reach your desired consistency—we like it soft with just a bit of crunch left. Season it all up with garlic and onion powder, and you've got a slightly sweet spaghetti marinara swap on your hands. Delicious!

Instant Soup Mix

Packets of powdered mix are great when all you've got on hand is hot water, a bowl, and a spoon. Plus, these are typically very low in calories—50 or less per serving. Asian options like miso and hot & sour are common, but you can also find basic veggie versions too.

HG Heads-Up

Don't get sucked in by instant soup cups or oversized packets that are mostly made up of noodles. Those are WAY high in calories!

Multi-tasking Food Find: Onion Soup Mix!

This stuff is incredible as a seasoning mix for so many things. Use it to flavor up your crumb coating when faux-frying. (See page 24 for the 411 on faux-frys!) Add it to ground meat (or soy crumbles). Mix it into fat-free plain Greek yogurt for a thick and flavor-packed veggie dip. The possibilities really are endless, so grab a packet and get goin'!

Low-Fat Turkey and Veggie Chili

Chili can sometimes be calorie dense, but it's also packed with filling fiber and protein. The fat and calorie counts can range from reasonable to excessive, so it is super-important to read those labels. And remember, if you're likely to have the full can at once, double those stats when considering them. Look for kinds with less than 200 calories and about 2 grams of fat per cup.

> **HG Standouts:** Amy's, Hormel, and Health Valley Organic.

FUN WITH . . . CANNED CHILI!

Pour it over a pile of chopped lettuce for a super-easy taco salad. Scoop some of the innards out of a leftover baked potato and fill it with this saucy stuff. Add a scoop to burgers and hot dogs (made with other guilt-free ingredients, of course) for a chili-topped fast-food fix. And see the TOP ATE list on the next page for more ideas!

Fat-Free Doesn't Always Say Fat-Free!
Low-Fat Won't Always Say Low-Fat!

As much as many companies love to splash impressive nutritional claims on product labels, it's not always the case . . . especially when things are naturally light, like basic broth and meatless chili. So flip those packages around. For chili to officially be considered low in fat by the FDA, it just needs to have 3 grams of fat or less per cup.

Fat-Free Chicken, Beef, and Vegetable Broth

Not only is broth great for making your own soups and stews, it's also CRUCIAL for making many other guilt-free goods. Use it when baking savory stuff to keep things moist without adding fat. Cook brown rice in broth instead of water to make it more flavorful. Or add a bit of cornstarch and your favorite spices, cook it in a small pot, and you've got a sauce, made to order!

HG Heads-Up

Think that low-sodium and reduced-sodium are the same thing? THINK AGAIN! Low-sodium broths will typically have around 140 milligrams of sodium per cup; reduced-sodium or less-sodium versions often still have over 500 milligrams a cup. It's a big reduction from the usual 900+ milligrams of sodium in standard broth, but they're DEFINITELY not the same product.

98% Fat-Free Cream of Celery, Chicken, and Mushroom Condensed Soups

These super-thick soups are crucial for making creamy comfort foods. Think chicken pot pie, tuna noodle casserole, green bean casserole . . . You get the picture! And use these soups as a rich sauce for things like baked chicken and skillet meals. A ½-cup serving goes a long way and will only add about 60 to 70 calories and 2.5 to 3 grams of fat.

~ BEANS ~

Canned beans are incredibly convenient and all-around impressive. While the canning process can diminish the nutrient value with some veggies, canned beans aren't any lower in nutrients than dried beans.

The Sodium Scenario

Rinsing them saves you about 20 percent of the sodium amount listed on the can. Look for no-salt-added beans and save another 500 milligrams or so per cup. Or go the middle route and get reduced-sodium varieties and rinse those. YAY!

The Bean Town Breakdown

As if tasting good weren't enough of a reason to chow down on your legumes . . .

* Beans are a good source of soluble AND insoluble fiber, both of which you need. FANTASTIC!

* They're full of complex carbs, which burn off slowly and keep you energized for a long time.

* Some of the other good things found in beans are folate, zinc, manganese, iron, and potassium. Woohoo!

* The average ½-cup serving of canned beans has 110 calories, half a gram of fat, 6 grams of fiber, and 7 grams of protein.

Black Beans

Use these for enchiladas, quesadillas, and more Mexican fare. Also great for Caribbean-inspired salads and slaws. An ideal ingredient for Spanish omelettes and scrambles, too!

Red Kidney Beans

Chili, gumbo, and southern comfort food are the places to use these beans. Like all beans, these rock in salads and slaws, and not just lettuce-based salads. Add them to scoopable salads and hearty veggie-based ones too.

Cannellini (a.k.a. White Kidney) Beans

These are creamy and mild and soft, making them ideal for purees and dips. Italian soup's another place that cannellinis taste yummy. For a schmancy salad, toss some with some tuna and light vinaigrette and serve it on a bed of greens.

Garbanzo Beans (a.k.a. Chickpeas)

These nutty beans taste great any time you want to bring Mediterranean or Greek inspiration to the table. Use them in salads, dips, stews, and soups. Want guilt-free hummus with a tangy twist? In a blender, combine rinsed and drained garbanzos with fat-free plain Greek yogurt, canned artichoke hearts (drained), and spices like cumin and garlic. Add a little broth, until it's smooth enough to blend, and you're done!

Fat-Free and Low-Fat Refried Beans

These mashed and seasoned beans are usually made from pintos. They're creamy and delicious in layered dips, burritos, taco salads, and more. Refried beans are even great as a straight dip for veggies. And there's no shortage of options on shelves. Traditional, vegetarian, black-bean-based, spicy, mild, etc. The stats do vary a bit, so look for those with around 110 calories per ½-cup serving.

See the Meat & Seafood section for info on canned tuna, salmon, chicken, and more!

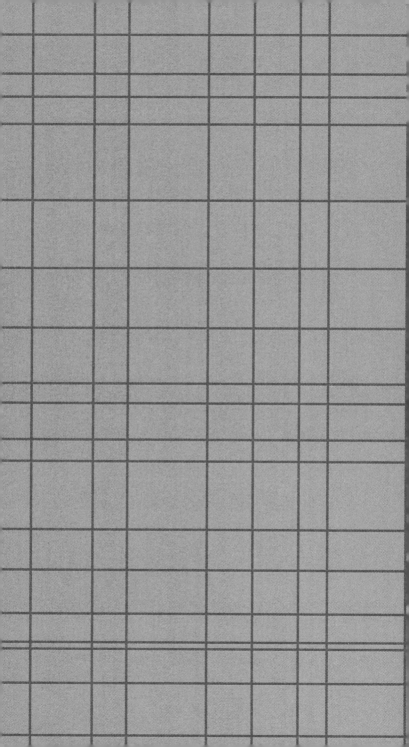

PACKAGED SNACKS

High-Fiber Crackers

When it comes to bite-sized crackers, look for ones with around 120 calories, 4 grams of fat or less, and a few grams of fiber per serving. And measure or count out your crackers before you eat them. Some of the many larger, flatbread-style crackers are great options. They make portion control much easier, and they're far more versatile. These are large, about 2 inches by 6 inches. There are super-light ones with about 35 calories each, as well as hearty types with around 100 calories per cracker.

HG Snack Ideas: The best thing about flatbread-style crackers? You can load them up with delicious items! Spread on some **Laughing Cow Light cheese**, and pile it high with lean deli slices. Top it with tuna and a slice of fat-free cheddar, and then toast it for a tuna melt! Add a smear of fat-free cream cheese and top with smoked salmon. Get creative with your crackers!

HG Heads-Up
Terms like "wheat" and "baked" don't necessarily mean high in fiber and low in fat. Read those labels!

Reduced-Fat Baked and Popped Potato Chips

Guilt-free potato chips have come a long way. There are air-popped chips that combine potato with other ingredients, like rice and corn. There are flavored varieties, everything from sea salt & vinegar to cheddar cheese. There are single-serving bags and stackable canisters (à la Pringles Light). Look for chips with about 120 calories, 4 grams of fat or less, and at least 1 gram of fiber per ounce. An ounce is usually equal to 15 to 20 chips.

HG All-Star!

Popchips! Never baked, never fried, these chips are POPPED. They taste delicious, come in lots of fun flavors, and are low in calories and fat. An ounce (about 20 chips) contains around 120 calories, 4 grams of fat, and a gram of fiber. They come in individual-serving bags as well as multi-serving bags. LOVE THESE!

HG Standouts: Kettle Brand Baked, Baked! Lay's, Pringles Light, and Cape Cod 40% Reduced Fat/Less Fat.

Amazing Chip Swap Alert!

These items make amazing chip alternatives when baked! Check 'em out . . .

6-Inch Corn Tortillas — Cut tortillas in half, then cut each half into 3 triangles. Lay triangles close together in a single layer on a baking sheet sprayed with nonstick spray. Mist with nonstick spray and sprinkle evenly with salt. Bake at 400 degrees until crispy, about 8 minutes, carefully flipping about halfway through bake time. Then EAT!

Kale — Lay kale leaves on a baking sheet sprayed with nonstick spray. Spritz with the spray and sprinkle with salt. Bake at 425 degrees until crispy, about 5 to 8 minutes. Enjoy!

Lavash Bread or Light Flatbread — Cut into squares and lay on a baking sheet sprayed with nonstick spray. Bake at 425 degrees until crispy, about 2 to 4 minutes. Tada!

See the Bread and Produce sections for more about these wonder foods . . .

Low-Fat Baked Tortilla Chips

Baked tortilla chips that are low in fat are amazing. Look for ones with about 120 calories and 3 grams of fat per ounce (15 chips or so). Baked corn chips are more common than baked flour tortilla chips, but either kind will do as long as the stats are impressive.

HG Heads-Up
While the calorie counts are similar, standard fried tortilla chips have twice as much fat! So make sure to get chips labeled "baked" and check the fat count on the back!

> **HG Standout:** Guiltless Gourmet Tortilla Chips. So many flavors, so little time . . .

Recipe Idea! For crispy snacks, crush up your favorite chips and crisps, and use them to create "faux-fried" baked goodies. Dip items like chicken breast strips and onion cut into rings into a little fat-free egg substitute, and then coat them in the crumbs. Bake and chew! For more on faux-frying, see page 24.

Hard Pretzels

Pretzels are crispy but not very filling. But if it's a carby, sometimes salty, dough-based crunch you're after, these'll do the trick. They're nearly fat-free—an ounce has about 120 calories and 1 gram of fat—but the calories can still add up fast. Your best bet is to either buy portion-controlled bags or portion out a large bag into single servings immediately.

HG Snack Ideas: Pair a serving with light cheese or something to dunk in (like mustard or a low-calorie creamy dip) to make it go further. Crush a few up and serve over light yogurt or ice cream for a sweet 'n salty fix!

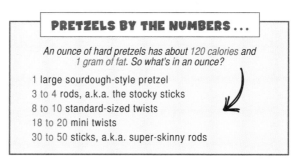

PRETZELS BY THE NUMBERS . . .

An ounce of hard pretzels has about 120 calories and 1 gram of fat. So what's in an ounce?

1 large sourdough-style pretzel
3 to 4 rods, a.k.a. the stocky sticks
8 to 10 standard-sized twists
18 to 20 mini twists
30 to 50 sticks, a.k.a. super-skinny rods

Fun Find: Pretzel Crisps, Thins, and Flats!

The latest shape of pretzels? FLAT. These pretzel snacks are nothing like regular pretzels. It's as if a giant tank came and steamrolled over regular pretzel twists. And the result is perfectly shaped, super-crunchy pretzels. We're not exactly sure why these things taste WAY better than regular pretzels, but they do. Have 10 to 12 for the usual stats. Many brands make them, but **Snack Factory** is the originator!

Rice Snacks and Soy Crisps

Here are a few underrated snack finds for you. These crunchy, slightly puffy treats come in a slew of great flavors. They're super-light, so you get a nice serving size for a reasonable number of calories. An ounce of either mini rice cakes or soy crisps has about 120 calories and 2 grams of fat, and you get about 15 pieces per ounce. Not bad! Look for sweet flavor options like chocolate and caramel. And scope out savory choices like BBQ and cheddar.

HG Snack Ideas: Crush up sweet types and sprinkle them over light ice cream, yogurt parfaits, and more. You can also make frozen mini sandwiches with some fat-free whipped topping as the creamy filling! Dip the savory types in guilt-free dips like salsa and fat-free sour cream, or break those into pieces and serve over chili, soup, and salad. So many options . . .

HG Standout: Quaker. A supermarket staple, you can usually find the Quaker Quakes lineup of decadent flavors. The serving size for these is an ounce, or about 15 mini cakes—each serving has about 120 calories and 2 grams of fat. Quaker also makes teenier versions called Mini Delights—those are drizzled with sweet topping and come in portion-controlled packs with 90 calories each!

Multi-Serving Snack Bag Alert!

No matter how impressive the stats are for a single serving, you need to consider the servings per bag and how likely you are to consume more than one serving. If a bag of chips lists eight 1-ounce servings, but you know you tend to go through it in four to five sittings, reconsider the REAL stats per serving! Ignorance is not bliss, people . . .

Rice Cakes

Rice cakes get a bad rap. Along with grapefruit and cottage cheese, they're considered "diet-y." Don't discount these large-and-in-charge snack cakes. They're light but crazy-low in calories, which means you can pile them high with other items. Plus, you're no longer limited to salted or unsalted. Like their little sisters, rice snacks, the full-sized treats come in a large array of flavors, from white cheddar to peanut butter & chocolate. Each rice cake has around 40 to 60 calories.

HG Snack Ideas: For a protein-packed snack, top one with salsa-fied tuna (that's salsa mixed with tuna) or light cheese and lean turkey. For a dessert fix, spread on a bit of peanut butter, pile on the banana slices, and finish it off with a nice squirt of **Reddi-wip**!

> **HG Standout:** Quaker. What can we say? They've got the crunchy rice snack market covered.

94% Fat-Free Microwave Popcorn Bags

Low-fat microwave popcorn is a terrific snack, because it's filling and you can eat a LOT of it. There are single-serving bags with around 100 calories and 2 grams of fat a pop (no pun intended), as well as multi-serving bags (great for sharing). The mini bags give you about 5 cups of popped corn, and the larger bags yield about 14 cups. There are classic flavors—butter, kettle corn, and lightly salted—as well as some fun varieties.

> **HG Standouts:** Jolly Time Healthy Pop, Orville Redenbacher's SmartPop!, and Pop Secret 100 Calorie Pop.

Pop-Up Popcorn Tip! Microwave a bag and take it into the movie theater with you—the popcorn there is not to be trusted!

HG Snack Idea: Toss some other bite-sized treats into your bowl of popcorn. Think freeze-dried fruit, cereal, a spoonful of mini chocolate chips . . . Just pay attention to what you're adding and don't overdo it! Or keep it simple and just sprinkle stuff on it, like cinnamon for a sweet fix or taco seasoning for some spice!

HG FYI:
If you do happen to eat an entire multi-serving bag of the stuff all by yourself, you'll only be taking in about 260 calories and 5 grams of fat. Not bad!

Decoding the
Popcorn Nutritional Panel

The serving size on a package of microwave popcorn will often be listed two ways: popped and unpopped. To further confuse things, companies sometimes list stats for one popped cup versus a serving of several popped cups. Here's the deal. The popped stats are what you want to pay attention to. A single cup of 94% fat-free popped corn has about 20 calories. A serving of about 5 cups will have about 100 calories, 2 grams of fat, 4 to 5 grams of fiber, and 3 to 4 grams of protein. The unpopped amount, listed in tablespoons, refers to the measured kernels themselves. And unless you're portioning out your kernels pre-popping, you don't need to pay attention to those stats!

Freeze-Dried Fruit

Freeze-dried fruit is fruit that's been zapped of its moisture, resulting in a light and crispy treat with a large serving size. Standard dried fruit, on the other hand, has been shriveled down to a tiny portion of its original size, resulting in a very small serving size. A ¼-cup serving of freeze-dried fruit contains about 25 calories. A ¼-cup serving of regular dried fruit clocks in with about 110 calories. In other words, you could eat a whole cup of the freeze-dried fruit before you even got close to the numbers on the conventionally dried stuff. YAY, VOLUME! Regular dried fruit, like raisins and dried cranberries, does come in handy for some baked goods and salads. But when it comes to assembling snack mixes, topping chilled treats, and straight-up snacking, go freeze-dried or go home.

The Usual (Delicious) Suspects: Strawberries, apples, and bananas are common freeze-dried fruit options. The occasional tropical find like mango or pineapple is always nice. And if you spy a fun mix like berries and bananas, it's your lucky day! Look for brands like Just Tomatoes, Etc.! in the produce or cereal aisle.

Unexpected Find: Gerber Graduates Mini Fruits! Why should babies have all the fun? This is one of the most common brands of freeze-dried fruit on shelves. As expected, they can be found in the baby foods aisle.

HG Heads-Up
Don't be fooled by apple chips or banana chips that have been oiled and fried. Just because they're crispy, that doesn't mean they're guilt-free. Always check ingredient lists and look for the magic word: freeze-dried.

> **HG Standout:** Funky Monkey. Clearly the most creative, clever, and delicious freeze-dried fruit snacks on the market today. LOVE those flavor combos . . . Bananamon! Pink Pineapple! Mmmmm . . .

100-Calorie Snack Packs & Treats

The market for portion-controlled, calorie-controlled treats has exploded in the past several years, which means there are many, MANY options. Some great and some not so great. Here's the scoop. Most 100-calorie snacks and packs are low in calories because the portion sizes are small. That's not to say they aren't useful. If there's something decadent you want to indulge in without going overboard (cookies, cake, chocolate-covered confections), the petite portion-controlled version can be a great option. There are some 100-calorie packs and treats that are actually lighter versions of a more fattening snack—those will give you a little more bang for your calorie buck. But in most cases, don't depend on these to fill you up if you're seriously hungry—they're better for satisfying a sugar craving or junk-food fix.

> **Think Outside the Pack!** In addition to trendy 100-calorie packs of cookies or chips, look for other snack treats with 100 calories or so. Single-serving bags of reduced-fat chips, 100-calorie bags of microwavable popcorn, and small-yet-satisfying pouches with 100 calories' worth of nuts.

> **HG Standouts:** Nabisco 100 Cal, Hostess 100 Calorie Packs, Entenmann's Little Bites, Kellogg's 100 Calorie Right Bites, **and** 100-calorie packs of Blue Diamond Almonds.

PROS & CONS OF
PORTION-CONTROLLED SNACKS

Obviously, single-serving snacks are ideal for tracking your fat and calorie intake. They save you the time and effort of counting out the appropriate amount of your treat of choice. Additionally, they're incredibly convenient since they're all wrapped up and ready to go with you anywhere. But portion-controlled snacks can be pricey. And your options are limited in terms of flavors and variety.

Bottom Line: If you can't be trusted around multi-serving snack bags and convenience is a top priority, choose individually packaged, calorie-controlled treats. If budget is the more important issue, go for the larger, less expensive packages with several servings.

DIY ALERT: Turn to page 111 for a huge and helpful guide to creating your own 100-calorie snacks. Save cents and increase your options. YES!!!

~ SNACK BARS ~

Cereal Bars & Chewy Granola Bars

Soft and tasty grain-based bars are great as an on-the-go snack or breakfast component. They usually have 90 to 140 calories, 2 to 5 grams of fat, and 3 to 4 grams of fiber. Some even pack in a few grams of protein. These are a great emergency snack to stash at work, in your car, wherever. If you're too hungry to wait until mealtime but only need a little something to take the edge off, stick with these as opposed to a higher-calorie, more substantial bar.

> **HG Standouts:** Quaker, Fiber One, and Special K each have a line of 90-calorie chewy bars in assorted flavors. All are delicious. **Kashi's Chewy Granola** and **Cereal bars** are each a little higher, with around 130 calories per bar; but they taste fantastic and are full of good-for-you ingredients.

Crunchy Granola Bars

These are the more dense, crispier, heartier granola bars that come two to a pack. They're more filling than their chewy counterparts and tend to be higher in protein. Look for twofers with about 180 calories, 6 grams of fat, 3 grams of fiber, and 5 grams of protein. Keep them handy in case you find yourself super-hungry and your next meal is nowhere in sight.

> **HG Standouts:** Nature Valley and Kashi TLC Crunchy Granola.

Decadent Snack Bars

Think of these as your candy bar replacement when the craving hits. They're fun and indulgent but not really filling. They hit the spot for a sweet craving. Look for kinds that ride the line between candy (chocolate, caramel, peanut butter) and cereal (oats and other grains). There are plenty out there with 150 calories and 5 grams of fat or less. They might pack a sizable amount of sugar, but they're likely to be less fat-packed and calorie-dense than actual candy bars.

> **HG Standouts:** Fiber One, Kellogg's FiberPlus, and Special K.

"Mini-Meal" Bars

These can be tricky. You want to avoid the full-on meal replacement bars—which can have 300+ calories—unless you're genuinely replacing breakfast, lunch, or dinner (or preparing to run a marathon!). Look for bars with 200 calories or less and sizable amounts of protein and fiber. Aim for at least 8 grams of protein and about 4 grams of fiber. Some bars are a bit lower in protein but pack a nice amount of healthy fats from things like nuts. Those are also good and satisfying—just keep an eye on the total calorie count. Like those crunchy granola bars, keep these around for when you need a hunger-buster on the go.

> **HG Standouts:** Kashi GoLean, Kind Bars, Luna Bars (and Luna Protein Bars), and Larabars.

~ NUTS ~

Best & Worst in a Nutshell

All nuts are not created equal . . .

The most-bang-for-your-calorie-buck award goes to . . . pistachios! Have around 40 kernels for about 160 calories.

The best-source-of-protein trophy goes to . . . peanuts! A whopping 7 grams in a 1-ounce serving (about 27 peanuts). That ounce also packs in 160 calories, 14 grams of fat, and about 2.5 grams of fiber.

Winning combo of fiber and protein? It's a tie: pistachios and almonds! Each ounce (about 24 almonds or 50 pistachios) packs 3 grams of fiber and 6 grams of protein. See more on these HG picks below and on the next page.

Two common nuts with unimpressive stats are walnuts and pecans. An ounce of walnuts (13 to 18 halves) has 185 calories and 18 grams of fat, and a 1-ounce serving of pecans (about 20 halves) has about 200 calories and 20 grams of fat.

Pistachios in the Shell

The reason pistachios in the shell are such a great snack is that they take a while to eat—it's like a little project prying 'em open! Once shelled, toss pistachios into your cereal or yogurt, top off salads with them, or eat them on their own. An ounce of these—about 40 kernels—has around 160 calories, 13 grams of fat, 3 grams of fiber, and 6 grams of protein.

Almonds: Whole and Sliced

Almonds are some of the most nutritious nuts around. They have vitamins, potassium, fiber, calcium, disease-battling phytonutrients . . . you name it. An ounce—about 24 almonds—has about 165 calories, 14 grams of fat, 3 grams of fiber, and 6 grams of protein. We recommend adding a quarter-ounce (about 6 nuts) here and there to salads, snack mixes, yogurt, and more.

Nutty-Good Find: All Natural Almond Accents!
This fantastic stuff is slivered super-thin . . . so a little goes a looooong way. In SEVEN rockin' flavors, they range from savory to sweet. A tablespoon has 40 calories, 3 to 3.5 grams of fat, 1 to 2 grams of carbs, and 1 gram of fiber.

Portion-Controlled Picks: 100-calorie packs of Blue Diamond and Emerald almonds! These
may very well be our favorite type of 100-calorie packs. They're an ideal emergency snack, they're travel-friendly, and they make portion control a snap. Look for seasoned options, too, like cocoa roasted and cinnamon dusted!

Tips & Tricks for Nut-Chewers!

* Either pick up portion-controlled packs or immediately divvy up your nuts into individual servings. Don't snack on 'em straight from a multi-serving bag or container—unless you have amazing self-control.

* If you're adding nuts to a meal or snack, crush 'em up to make them go a lot further. Or opt for thinly sliced when buying.

* Go for nuts still in their shells. They take longer to eat, so you'll fill up before you eat too many.

* Avoid heavily honey-coated or candy-coated nuts. Who needs the extra calories?

* Mix your favorite nuts up with freeze-dried fruit and/or light puffy cereal for a fun trail-mix-like snack.

* Choose nuts that are dry-roasted or raw. No extra oils necessary!

Jerky is one of the best emergency snack foods. Travel-ready snacks that are this packed with protein (and so low in fat) are hard to find. Not a meat eater? Go for soy jerky! Look for options with 80 calories or less per serving. There's a whole world of jerky out there, so find kinds you love and stock up!

HG Standouts: Jack Link's, Tillamook Country Smoker, Tasty Eats (non-chicken flavors), and Oh Boy! Oberto.

HG Heads-Up
See the TOP ATE Items Worth Ordering Online section on page 199 for the full 411 on another favorite!

LABEL ALERT!
What's More Accurate:
The Quantity or the Weight?

Nutritional panels often list both, but the weight is almost always the most accurate measurement. This is especially true of foods that have many pieces per serving, like bite-sized crackers and mini cookies. If you read labels carefully, you'll see that many products own up to the fact that a serving consists of "about" X number of chips, cookies, pieces, etc. The weight—which is sometimes given in grams instead of ounces—is more exact. Other snack packages give a precise quantity, but if you're skeptical, weigh the supposed amount in a serving and see how it compares to the weight given on the package. One more thing: Big-name brands are more likely to be accurate in their estimates, while mom 'n pop companies can be less reliable.

DIY 100-CALORIE PACKS
MAKE A SOLO SNACK OR MIX 'N MATCH...

14 almonds (dry roasted)
100 calories, 9g fat, 3g carbs, 2g fiber, 0.5g sugars, 3.5g protein

25 pistachios (dry roasted)
100 calories, 8g fat, 5g carbs, 1.5g fiber, 1g sugars, 3g protein

16 Popchips (average of all flavors)
100 calories, 3g fat, 16g carbs, 1g fiber, 1g sugars, 1g protein

15 Guiltless Gourmet Tortilla Chips (average of all flavors)
100 calories, 2g fat, 17.5g carbs, 1.5g fiber, 0g sugars, 1.5g protein

40 small hard pretzel sticks
100 calories, 0g fat, 23g carbs, 1g fiber, 1g sugars, 2g protein

19 mini hard pretzel twists
100 calories, <0.5g fat, 20.5g carbs, <1g fiber, <0.5g sugars, 1.5g protein

5 cups popped 94% fat-free microwave popcorn
100 calories, 0.5g fat, 22g carbs, 4g fiber, 0g sugars, 2.5g protein

13 Quaker Quakes Rice Snacks (average of all flavors)
100 calories, 2g fat, 19.5g carbs, 0g fiber, 3.5g sugars, 1.5g protein

4 Hershey's Milk Chocolate Kisses
100 calories, 5.5g fat, 10.5g carbs, <0.5g fiber, 9g sugars, 1g protein

4 teaspoons mini semi-sweet chocolate chips
100 calories, 5.25g fat, 12g carbs, 0.5g fiber, 10.5g sugars, 1g protein

27 Reese's Pieces
100 calories, 4.5g fat, 12g carbs, 0.5g fiber, 10g sugars, 2g protein

45 mini marshmallows
100 calories, 0g fat, 25.5g carbs, 0g fiber, 18g sugars, 0.5g protein

¼ cup sweetened dried cranberries
100 calories, <0.5g fat, 26.5g carbs, 2.5g fiber, 21.5g sugars, 0g protein

25 small jelly beans
100 calories, 0g fat, 25g carbs, 0g fiber, 20g sugars, 0g protein

BREAD

Light Bread Slices

Not every loaf slapped with a "light" label is a good guilt-free pick. Look for those with high fiber counts and 40 to 45 calories per slice.

BREAD

HG Heads-Up
A typical serving has anywhere from 1 to 3 slices. So read labels carefully and do the math!

HG Tip: If you're craving a certain bread type, like rye or sourdough, that isn't offered in light varieties, look for thinly sliced loaves with the fewest calories per slice.

> **HG Standouts:** Weight Watchers, Nature's Own Double Fiber, Arnold Bakery Light, Sara Lee Delightful, and Pepperidge Farm (Light Style, Very Thin, and Whole Grain).

FUN WITH . . . SLICED BREAD!
In addition to standard sandwiches, try these ideas out . . .

Grilled 'Wiches. A little light whipped butter or light buttery spread goes a long way. Spread a bit on the outside of your sandwich (half a tablespoon on each side!), and then cook in a skillet or a grill pan. Toasty, tasty, awesome!

French Toast. Dip your slices in fat-free egg substitute and then sprinkle with cinnamon before lightly cooking in a skillet—dust with a teaspoon of powdered sugar and serve with sugar-free pancake syrup!

EZ Baked Croutons. If you're really craving the buttery, seasoned crunch of croutons, avoid the fattening kinds on shelves and make your own! Cut slices of light bread into small squares and place on a baking sheet sprayed with nonstick spray. Spritz with zero-calorie butter spray and sprinkle with garlic powder. Bake in the oven at 350 degrees until crispy, about 4 minutes. Tada!

~ BUNS ~

Light and High-Fiber Hamburger Buns

The key here is to avoid oversized rolls. Those can easily contain 200 calories or more. Look for 80-calorie light buns or standard (small-ish) ones with about 110 calories. These fluffy rolls are ideal for classic burgers made with guilt-free patties, and they're great for backyard BBQs.

> **HG Standouts:** Sara Lee Delightful, Nature's Own Double Fiber, and Pepperidge Farm Classic.

HG All-Star!
100-Calorie Flat Sandwich Buns

While standard burger buns do have their time and place, these slim trendsetters are a welcome addition to market aisles. Face it: Bread's main purpose is to hold your sandwich filling. You don't need all the extra carby calories that come with *super-doughy* buns and breads. And since these thin rolls have more surface area than others, you can layer on more delicious and filling goodies. In addition to their impressive 100-calorie price tag, these typically contain a good amount of fiber. For panini-style sandwiches, grill these in a skillet once assembled.

> **HG Standouts:** Arnold Select/Oroweat Sandwich Thins, Pepperidge Farm Deli Flats, and Nature's Own Sandwich Rounds.

HG Heads-Up
Some "flats" have much higher stats than others, so read labels carefully . . . don't get faked out!

Light and High-Fiber Hot Dog Buns

Like regular burger buns, your best option is to stick with light ones that contain around 80 calories. However, high-fiber options with around 110 calories are also good choices. Pair these with guilt-free hot dogs (the full 411 on those can be found on page 38) and all your favorite extras.

> **Recipe Idea!** Get crazy with hot dog buns and use them to make stuffed French toast nuggets! Just fill one with low-sugar fruit preserves and spreadable cheeses, and then gently slice it into chunks. Lightly coat with fat-free liquid egg substitute and cook in a skillet until browned on all sides. YUM and FUN!

HG Standouts: Sara Lee Delightful, Nature's Own Double Fiber, and Pepperidge Farm Classic.

FOOD FAKER ALERT!

Watch out for over-caloried "wheat" bread products posing as good-for-you options. "Whole grain" and "whole wheat" are better indicators of a nutritious choice. But when in doubt, check the calorie and fiber counts!

BREAD

~ ENGLISH MUFFINS ~

Light English Muffins

Obsessed with nooks and crannies? These are for you. They're excellent bread and bun swaps, since it's incredibly easy to find fiber-packed options with about 100 calories. Great for breakfast sandwiches and open-faced melts. Their unique texture makes them a fun addition for unconventional casseroles and stuffings—just be sure to keep the other ingredients guilt-free!

> **HG Standouts:** Thomas', Western Bagel Alternative, and Weight Watchers.

~ PITAS ~

Light and High-Fiber Pitas

Pita pockets are fantastic because you can tear off one end and pack them full of stuff, or you can halve them and fill each half individually. They can easily rip, though, so it's best to warm them slightly before stuffing. You can even use one as a nice 'n sturdy pizza bottom—it's especially great for Greek-style pizzas with fat-free or reduced-fat feta! Look for pitas with 125 calories or less. Those labeled "whole wheat" often have the higher fiber counts.

> **HG Standouts:** Western Bagel Alternative and Weight Watchers.

BREAD

Large High-Fiber Flour Tortillas with About 110 Calories Each

Large tortillas can be a great alternative to sliced bread. Wraps are capable of holding much more of the satisfying sandwich fillers. The trick is to keep an eye on calorie counts and look for high-fiber options. And make sure the size is realistic—8 inches or larger—so that you can effectively pile on or wrap up your goodies. Like pitas, you'll want to warm these slightly before you go bending and folding.

BREAD

Recipe Ideas! These tortillas are beyond perfect for whipping up Mexican-inspired treats—quesadillas, wraps, burritos, etc.—and so much more! But if you think a tortilla is just for Mexican food, think again! When baked whole, it can become thin pizza crust. Slice it into triangles and then bake until crispy for high-fiber tortilla chips. Use as a wrap stuffed with breakfast goodies, lean meats, veggies, light cheeses . . . whatever!

HG All-Star!

La Tortilla Factory Smart & Delicious Low Carb High Fiber Large Tortillas! Each of these has just 80 calories and 3 grams of fat, plus a whopping 12 grams of fiber and 8 grams of protein! La Tortilla Factory also makes 100 Calorie Tortillas that are equally impressive, so look for those as well.

HG Standouts: Mission Carb Balance Tortillas, Tumaro's 8-Inch Healthy Tortillas, and Tumaro's 8-Inch Low in Carbs Tortillas.

Light High-Fiber Flatbreads

These are super-similar to flour tortillas, just larger and rectangular. They're perfect for making large wraps and thin-crust pizzas. In fact, they can be used almost anywhere large tortillas can. Look for those with 110 calories or less.

HG All-Star!

Flatout Light! These 90-calorie items come in a slew of great flavors and they taste fantastic. The Traditional line is a little higher in calories, with about 130 per flatbread, but still completely respectable for an oversized bread option!

Hungry Girl Exclusive!
Flatout Foldit Flatbreads

These unique, figure-eight-shaped bread items are fluffier than tortillas but flatter than thin sandwich buns. Just fold one around your sandwich fillers of choice and CHEW. Each low-fat flatbread has 90 to 100 calories and 3 to 7 grams of fiber. We love these so much, we worked with Flatout to make them HG exclusive products. Pssst . . . Look for the Sliders version too: Only 140 calories for a 3-slider flatbread!

6-Inch Corn Tortillas

While high-fiber flour tortillas are better basics, these smaller corn tortillas are great for Mexican treats like taquitos, fajitas, and even crunchy baked corn chips. They often come in both yellow and white—the yellow flats have a more grainy, authentic texture, while the white types are smoother with a less prominent flavor. Look for ones with 60 calories or less. Use the slightly larger ones with 70 to 80 calories for making enchiladas.

~ TACO SHELLS ~

Corn Taco Shells

These are fun for crunchy tacos and surprisingly reasonable in the stats department. Store-bought versions are more often baked than fried, which is why they're not too high in calories and fat. Look for standard-sized (not jumbo) shells with around 60 calories, 2 grams of fat, and 1 gram of fiber each.

> **Fun Find!** If you can get your hands on some flat-bottomed taco shells, DO IT. They're easier to assemble and you can usually stuff even more guilt-free goodies inside!

> **Recipe Ideas!** Don't feel bound by traditional taco uses! Fill your shells with egg scrambles, grilled veggies, deli-style salads, lean meats, and more.

BREAD

~ BAGELS ~

Light Bagels

Look for light bagel items with no more than 150 calories and 1 gram of fat each. Bonus points if they pack in some fiber. There are mini options, too, with 100 calories or so; those are fun, but not hugely satisfying . . . Keep that in mind before you buy a bag and down six minis in one sitting!

Fun Find! Thomas' Bagel Thins.

These are like the flat sandwich buns of the bagel world. Each one contains an impressively low 110 calories and an impressively high 4 to 5 grams of fiber.

HG SHOCKER!

> The average store-bought bagel contains around
> **300 calories** . . . and that's before you put anything on it!

HG Tips! If you can't find bagels with reasonable calorie counts, just get the lowest-calorie ones you can find. Then scoop out the insides before eating 'em—fewer calories and more room for delicious fillings! And don't forget to use guilt-free toppings like low-sugar or sugar-free jam, light spreadable cheese, and light whipped butter or light buttery spread.

> **HG Standouts:** Western Bagel Alternative and Weight Watchers.

Pillsbury Crescent Recipe Creations Seamless Dough Sheet

BREAD

Want pastries? Roll the dough around sweet stuff before baking. Need rolls? Too easy. Quickie starters? No prob. There's practically NOTHING this dough can't do . . . A serving is ⅛ᵗʰ of the package and has 120 calories and 6 grams of fat—but you can get as many as 12 servings out of it, depending on what you're making. Find it in the refrigerated section of the supermarket. It's all wrapped up in a cylindrical tube.

> **INSIDE INFO!** This is basically the same exact dough that's perforated and packaged as Reduced Fat Crescent Rolls, even though the package doesn't tout it as such (because the serving sizes differ). How 'bout that?!

Recipe Idea! When this dough gets together with a 12-cup muffin pan, fun is SURE to follow. Think of 'em as party planners. Roll out the dough sheet, and cut it into 12 squares. Spritz your pan with nonstick spray, and press a square of dough into each cup. Fill those dough cups with almost anything you like, and bake at 375 degrees until golden brown, about 12 to 15 minutes. (If your filling is raw, make sure it can be fully cooked in that amount of time.) AMAZING. You can also cook the soft shells up solo, and fill 'em up later with goodies. And each delicious doughy cup itself has just 60 calories and 3 grams of fat. NICE!

Pillsbury Classic Pizza Crust Dough

This refrigerated pizza crust dough in a can RULES. It is PERFECT for making no-guilt pizza for a crowd. And even though it says it makes 6 servings—each with 160 calories and 2 grams of fat—you can easily roll it out nice and thin and get 8 sizable servings out of it. In addition to pizza, you can use this dough to make breadsticks, big baked flatbreads . . . even calzones! See the Pizza Essentials section on **page 204** for more must-haves.

Pizza Crust Alternatives!
Unconventional pizza bottom alert!

Use high-fiber tortillas and flatbreads (just bake until crispy), light English muffins and pitas (toasted), and veggies like bell peppers (sliced and baked), eggplant (sliced and grilled), and portabella mushroom caps (baked or grilled) as pizza crusts. You can even use chicken cutlets that have been pounded thin as a protein-rich pizza bottom!

Lavash Bread

Lavash is a soft, thin Middle Eastern flatbread—it's kind of like a rectangular tortilla, but it's larger and a little thinner. If you don't see lavash in the bread aisle of the supermarket, look for it near the bakery or in the ethnic foods aisle. Any brand is fine, just check the stats—a large one should have about 100 calories, and the super-large ones should have around 200 calories. Here's an important tip, though: Since the sheets of lavash bread are larger than most bread products, the "serving size" may be for only HALF of one. So read the labels carefully. Use lavash as you would tortillas and flatbreads.

> **Recipe Idea!** We like to use lavash bread as a chip swap. Just cut the lavash bread into a total of 24 squares, each about 2 inches by 2 inches, and place on a baking sheet sprayed with nonstick spray. Bake in the oven at 425 degrees until crispy, about 2 to 3 minutes. That's it!

Ready-Made Dessert Crepes

These are, oddly enough, often found in the produce aisle, and they're amazing. They're super-thin, slightly sweet sheets that are incredible bases for blintzes, crepes, and pretty much anything sweet you want wrapped up in deliciousness. Fill them with pudding, fruit, yogurt, or any combination. Then you can (carefully) cook them in a skillet, freeze them for chilly treats, or enjoy them as is. Look for ones with about 50 calories and 1 gram of fat each.

> **HG Standouts:** Frieda's and Melissa's. Those ladies know their crepes. Both brands rock.

See also . . .

Fiber One Original bran cereal in the Cereal section . . . ground up and spiced, it's an amazing high-fiber breadcrumb swap!

FROZEN MEALS
AND MEAL STARTERS

Frozen Meals at a Glance

Food from the freezer aisle is a part of life for most people. When you're in a hurry, it can be a much better option than fast food or takeout. The higher the fiber and protein amounts, the more filling these picks will be. You'll have the most luck if you seek out brands or lines known for their diet-friendly options. Words like light and lean will steer you in the right direction, but always check the nutritional info on individual items. And be sure to scope out the **TRIO of Frozen Meal Companions** and **Guide to Supersizing Frozen Meals** in this section, for tips on maximizing your freezer-aisle satisfaction!

~ BREAKFAST FINDS ~

Low-Fat Waffles

When choosing frozen waffles, look for ones with about 160 calories, 3 grams of fat or less, and at least 3 grams of fiber per two-waffle serving—that's only 80 calories or so per waffle!

Snack & Meal Ideas! Enjoy an unconventional open-faced sandwich by piling one high with things like lean ham, egg scrambles, light cheese, and more. For a hearty grab-n-go meal fix, take two and make a full-on sandwich!

HG Standouts: Kashi GoLean, Eggo Low Fat, and Van's Lite.

Breakfast Sandwiches, Bowls, and Wraps

With these, it's all about convenience. You'll have a lot more options (and probably better stats) if you assemble one yourself from items found in other sections of this book. But these are definitely a fantastic alternative to most drive-thru breakfast options. Look for choices under 300 calories and with 10 grams of fat or less. Seek out selections boasting egg whites, turkey sausage, turkey bacon, and low-fat egg scrambles.

Fun Find: Kraft Bagel-fuls! These are like the bagel versions of Twinkies. Each cream-cheese-stuffed treat contains an impressive 200 calories and 5 grams of fat or less, plus a couple of grams of fiber and a handful of protein grams.

More Fun Finds: Oatmeal Bowls! A few brands make freezer-aisle versions of hot cereal. Expect big fiber counts . . . but we recommend adding fruit to fill out the grains!

HG Standouts: Weight Watchers Smart Ones Morning Express, Jimmy Dean D-Lights Breakfast Sandwiches and Bowls, and Cedarlane Egg White Omelettes and Breakfast Burritos.

HG All-Star!
Vitalicious VitaTops

If sweet baked goods are your downfall, get better acquainted with these 100-calorie (or less) muffin tops. These are high-fiber, low-fat, all-natural, and all-around amazing treats. You can find limited varieties at select markets, usually chocolate flavors, but they're worth seeking out. Pair one with a piece of fruit for a quick breakfast. Read more about these in the Frozen Desserts section.

FROZEN MEALS AND MEAL STARTERS

Flatbreads, Panini, and Pocket Sandwiches

Cheesy, toasty, meaty . . . Think of them as decadent swaps for fast-food and fatty sandwich-shop fare. There are two types in this category—meal replacements and snacks. The best way to identify the difference? THE STATS. Anything between 250 and 350 calories is more of a meal replacement. An item with 150 to 240 calories or so is more of a snack. Either way, opt for those with 10 or fewer fat grams and several grams of fiber and protein.

HG Standouts: Amy's, Lean Pockets, Lean Cuisine, and Weight Watchers Smart Ones.

HG Tip: Look carefully, and you'll find some impressive options that aren't marketed as diet-friendly. For example, some Hot Pockets are completely reasonable in terms of fat and calories. So bundle up and spend some time perusing the frozen foods aisle!

Burritos and Wraps

For these handheld frozen meals, 350 calories and around 10 grams of fat is a good ceiling to abide by. If you plan to plate one, salsa and fat-free sour cream are great toppings; serve it over shredded lettuce for a little fresh crunch! Pay attention to size as well as stats. The bonus to choosing these types of frozen foods is that it's easier to gauge their size. If the calorie and fat counts are approaching that top limit, make sure it isn't some tiny snack wrap.

HG Standouts: Amy's and Cedarlane.

FROZEN MEALS AND MEAL STARTERS

~ PIZZA ~

Multi-Serving Pizzas

SERVING-SIZE ALERT! Most multi-serving pizzas in the freezer aisle supposedly contain THREE servings. This is one of those scenarios where it's extremely important to consider what a realistic serving size is for you. Are you likely to serve yourself a third . . . and then later finish off one half of the pie? If so, do the math before you buy. Look for pies with around 240 to 270 calories and 10 grams of fat or less per serving.

> **HG Standouts:** Kashi's options feature amazingly crispy thin crust, really unique toppings, and rich and tasty sauces. Go, Kashi! **Amy's** has crazy-cool crusts and decadent flavors; just check the nutritional panels, because not all of these are guilt-free.

Pizza at a Glance . . .

Keywords to Embrace:
Thin crust, whole grain, and veggie lovers.

Words to Avoid:
Deep dish, stuffed crust, and any-number meat (like "three meat" or more!).

FROZEN MEALS AND MEAL STARTERS

Single-Serving Pizzas

If you're dining solo, individual pies are your best bet. Acceptable options range from 300 to 400 calories and have 5 to 10 grams of fat. Why are higher calorie counts okay here? Because unlike those multi-serving pies, once you're done, you're done. Some of these crisp up nicely in the microwave while others require you to fire up that oven. There are so many choices in this category and, again, since you don't have to do any fancy math or worry about overdoing it, you can have fun when choosing flavor options. There are French bread styles, wood-fired flavors, and schmancy café-inspired pizzas. Yum!

HG Alternative! Those frozen flatbread sandwiches? They frequently come not-yet-folded, so you can consume them flat like pizza instead!

HG Standouts: Lean Cuisine, Weight Watchers Smart Ones, and Amy's.

~ ENTRÉES ~

A TRIO of Frozen Meal Companions ...

Frozen dinners can be on the small side and sometimes not satisfying enough on their own. But before you double up and down TWO (thus consuming twice the calories), consider these three fantastic sides ...

1. Salad. Dump some bagged lettuce in a bowl and enjoy with your favorite guilt-free dressing on the side. Just remember: Dip, don't pour!

2. Broth-Based Soup. It's true what they say: People who start a meal with broth-based soup consume fewer calories overall. Grab a spoon and start slurping!

3. Crunchy Cut-Up Veggies. Face it: We often turn to frozen meals because we're STARVING and don't have time for much else. So instead of munching on chips and cookies out of desperation while you wait for the microwave to beep, chomp on baby carrots and red bell pepper strips instead.

Classic Trays

Try to stay at around 350 calories and no more than 10 grams of fat here. Look for ones with impressive amounts of protein, plenty of veggies (although you can always add more), and not too much starch (pasta, rice, potatoes, etc.).

> **HG Standouts:** Kashi, Healthy Choice, Lean Cuisine, Cedarlane, Organic Bistro, Amy's, and Morningstar Farms.

HG Tip: Even with your favorite brands, pay attention to stats. Not every entrée is a good choice if you're watching your calorie intake.

Steam-Ready Selections

Frozen veggies kicked off the steam-in-the-bag trend, and now full-on entrées have followed suit. We like this because the steamable bowls and bags tend to contain more veggies and protein than limited-space trays.

HG Heads-Up
Beware of two-serving and three-serving bags if you're eating for one!

> **HG Standouts:** Lean Cuisine Market Creations and Healthy Choice Café Steamers.

FROZEN MEALS AND MEAL STARTERS

SUPER-SPECIFIC
STANDOUTS

*Some frozen selections are so special,
they need their very own section . . .*

Amy's Mexican Tamale Pie
An unbelievably delicious, authentic Mexican treat consisting of a yummy mix of pinto beans, corn, zucchini, and crushed tomatoes—topped with a light polenta. With only 150 calories, this low-fat, high-fiber, personal-sized pie makes a perfect snack or meal starter. Excellent!

Kashi Mayan Harvest Bake
This is arguably the best frozen dinner of all time. It's full of incredible items like sweet potatoes, black beans, and plantains. It's loaded with grains and pumpkin seeds. And it's smothered with a sweet, smoky, incredible sauce. All that and it's filling and delicious for under 350 calories!

Amy's Cheese Pizza Toaster Pops
Here we have a 160-calorie snack that's basically a pizza-packed Pop-Tart. No, it's not a sweet pastry; it's a toastable, savory treat filled with tasty tomato sauce and gooey cheese. Find it. Eat it. Love it.

Contessa Stir-Fry Meals
These straight-to-stove entrées have no starchy noodles, rice, or pasta—just tons of protein and veggies with sauce that comes on the side! They contain 2 to 3 servings, but the stats are so impressive—around 180 calories and 3 grams of fat per serving—you could eat the whole thing without doing much damage!

Amy's Shepherd's Pie
Yup, another amazing option from Amy's. This meat-free treat is full of seasoned veggies and beans and topped with a creamy smashed potato crust. Yum! Even major carnivores won't miss the beef. This is crazy-good, guilt-free comfort food. And the single-serving pie has just 160 calories and 4 grams of fat.

Honorable Mentions!
Kashi Mexicali Black Bean Stone-Fired Thin Crust Pizza
Healthy Choice Pumpkin Squash Ravioli
Lean Cuisine Market Creations Chicken Margherita
Morningstar Farms Lasagna with Sausage-Style Crumbles
Healthy Choice Steaming Entrées Honey Balsamic Chicken
Lean Cuisine Spa Cuisine Roasted Honey Chicken

HG's Guide
to Supersizing Frozen Meals!

Veggies are a FANTASTIC way to add volume and fiber to your frozen entrée of choice. There's typically PLENTY of sauce to go around. The key is to select the best veggies for the job . . .

Asian-Style Entrées — Steamed bean sprouts and steamed broccoli work well with most Chinese dishes. And skillet-cooked or steamed broccoli cole slaw is a terrific addition to lo mein and other Asian noodle dishes.

Pasta Meals — Use a veggie peeler to create thin ribbons of zucchini; then boil or steam and add to fettuccine dinners! Spaghetti squash—baked or steamed—is ideal in any kind of spaghetti meal. And don't miss the Add These Anywhere options below . . .

Pizza, Pizza — Pile your pizza high with extra veggies like sliced mushrooms, thinly sliced onion, bell pepper strips, and spinach. You can toss these right on top of your frozen pizza before cooking it up. Crushed red pepper won't add volume, but the spiciness should slow you down and keep you from inhaling too many slices!

Beef-Based Options — While your beef entrées are being nuked, toss a sliced portabella cap in a skillet to bulk things up. For ground-meat meals, add chopped mushrooms to that skillet instead. You get extra flavor for hardly any calories at all.

Mexican-Style Selections — Cook up fajita-style veggies, like onions and bell peppers, on the stove to fill out your frozen fiesta. And stewed tomatoes are great over anything Mexican!

. . . .

Add These Anywhere!

Frozen Veggies — These are as easy to prep as frozen dinners, and they come in tons of varieties so you can pick one that goes well with your meal. In fact, get in the habit of picking out frozen veggies to go with your entrées in the same shopping trip.

House Foods Tofu Shirataki Noodles — Another item that can go into practically any type of frozen meal. Just drain, rinse, microwave, and dry as thoroughly as possible (that last step cannot be overemphasized . . . DRY THEM!)—then stir 'em into your meal of choice. You'll add volume to your meal for only 40 calories per bag of noodles! Turn to **page 189** for more about these special noodles.

See also . . .

> * The Meat and Seafood section! * The Meat Substitutes section! *
> * The Frozen Vegetables in the Produce section! *

ICE CREAM & FROZEN DESSERTS

~ ICE CREAM ~

HG Heads-Up: Deceptive Attention-Getters!

* No Sugar Added!   * Sherbet!
* Frozen Yogurt!   * Non-Dairy!
* All Natural!   * Made with Real Fruit!
* Sorbet!

In the ice cream aisle, you'll see claims and product names like these. If you're watching your sugar, avoiding artificial ingredients, or are allergic to dairy, a few of these can be very helpful. But it's important to realize that none of these implies a correlation with low calorie counts! Words like "light" and "reduced-fat" will lead you in the right direction, but you still need to read those labels to be sure.

Light and Fat-Free Ice Cream Cartons

Look for products that have around 130 calories and 4 grams of fat per ½-cup serving. The fat-free types have fewer calories, but your flavor options are usually limited and the light stuff is a lot richer in taste. There are some ice creams out there that pack a few grams of fiber. Added fiber is always nice, but don't expect these fiber-infused dairy desserts to fill you up the same way a bowl of raspberry-topped bran cereal would. (They won't.)

Supersize It! Since the serving size for ice cream in a tub is relatively small, plan to supersize your scoop with fun extras that are low in calories. Add a generous squirt of Fat Free Reddi-wip, or top off your treat with a serving of Cool Whip Free. Toss some mixed berries into your dessert bowl. Add a few mini marshmallows. Put that scoop of ice cream in a blender with light vanilla soymilk and crushed ice—then blend away for a freezy-good shake!

HG Standout: Dreyer's/Edy's Slow Churned Light. The D/E peeps know their stuff. This ever-expanding line of light ice cream contains half the fat of regular ice cream, plus ⅓rd fewer calories. But all that would mean nothing if it weren't for the fact that this is some of the richest, creamiest stuff in the frozen desserts aisle. It's delicious and comes in amazing flavors, each with 100 to 130 calories and 3 to 6 grams of fat per serving. BTW, other ice cream containers that call out "half churned" or "double churned" typically contain half the fat of regular ice cream as well!

PORTION DISTORTION!
HALF-CUP SERVING?!

Possibly the most unrealistic of serving sizes, a portion of ice cream is only ½ cup. It's not a lot. Try measuring it out and see—it's MUCH less than anything you'd get at an ice cream shop. Think you're serving-size savvy? We put HG staffers, friends, and family members to the test to see how closely they could estimate a serving size. Here's what we found . . .

* The average estimation among participants was 20 percent more than ½ cup!

* The more the ice cream softened, the more people overestimated their portions. That ½-cup serving is based on lightly packed ice cream, people, so keep that in mind!

* Those portioning out plain vanilla ice cream over-scooped by MORE than those working with chunky cookie dough ice cream. Perhaps we're more cautious with decadent stuff?

Bottom Line: If you know you're likely to eat a full cup each time you enjoy it, double those stats while you're still in the freezer aisle to make sure they work for you . . . And if you don't want to spend 200+ calories for an ice cream fix, stick with portion-controlled treats.

Portion-Controlled
Cups of Light Ice Cream

Since it's so easy to go overboard with ice cream, single-serving cups are a great thing. Sure, these individual containers may cost more than the cartons, but they'll likely stop you from consuming way too much ice cream. Look for cups that are about 4 ounces in size with around 150 calories and 3 grams of fat each.

HG Heads-Up:
Not Everything Small in Size Is Low in Calories!
The brands that make super-fattening gourmet ice cream have mini cups too, and those can pack quite a fat 'n calorie punch—as much as 250 calories and 15 grams of fat for a measly 3½ ounces of ice cream!

Another HG Heads-Up:
Beware of 2-Serving Containers!
There are a few dual-serving tubs in the aisles whose labels might lead you to believe there's only 100 calories or so inside. Check the servings per container, people! Don't assume . . .

HG Standouts: Skinny Cow, Weight Watchers, and Dreyer's/Edy's.

HG Trick!

For a fruity syrup that isn't loaded with calories and sugar, just place a spoonful of low-sugar or sugar-free fruit preserves in a microwave-safe bowl along with a teaspoon of water. Microwave just until warm (a few seconds), and stir until a syrup-like consistency is reached. Yay!

ICE CREAM SWAPARAMA!

Frozen Cool Whip Free!

This is a fantastic stand-in for vanilla ice cream. While we wouldn't fill a dessert bowl with it and grab a spoon, we recommend adding a frozen scoop to diet soda for a low-cal float and making faux ice cream sandwiches with rice cakes or low-fat graham cracker squares—just use thawed whipped topping and then freeze the whole "sandwich!" Fun, fun, fun . . .

Frozen Fruit in the Blender!

For smoothies and shakes, the creamy texture of frozen banana is amazing. Berries, peaches, and mangos work in blended drinks too. Another cool trick? Blend up partially thawed super-sweet fruit—like the three just mentioned—on its own, or with a very small amount of a light juice drink, for a sorbet-like treat!

Fat-Free Yogurt, Frozen!

No, we don't mean standard fro yo bought by the tub. We mean refrigerated fat-free yogurt—like Yoplait Light—that's been frozen for a chilly and super-creamy treat! For best results, don't let it freeze entirely. (You might break a spoon that way.) Or let it thaw for five to ten minutes if it's been fully frozen. Another fun idea? Mix some thawed Cool Whip Free with the yogurt before freezing. It'll taste even more like ice cream that way!

Don't miss the frozen fruit fun on page 76!

Light and Low-Fat Ice Cream Bars

As if ice cream couldn't get any better, someone went and put it on a stick. (We all know food on a stick is fun!) These are often more decadent than a single scoop, with chocolatey coatings and cookie crumbles, and they've got the whole portion-control thing working for them! Look for bars with 150 calories and 5 grams of fat or less.

> **HG Standouts:** Skinny Cow (especially Truffle Bars!) and **Breyers Smooth & Dreamy**.

Low-Fat Ice Cream Sandwiches

Another super selection in the portion-controlled arena: light ice cream surrounded by a pair of soft cookie-like wafers. These are sometimes round, sometimes rectangular, and come in a bunch of great flavor combos, like chocolate wafers with peanut butter ice cream. Mmmm! Look for options with about 150 calories and 3 grams of fat.

> **HG Standouts:** Skinny Cow and **Weight Watchers**.

ICE CREAM & FROZEN DESSERTS

Light and Low-Fat Ice Cream Cones

Look for sugar cones filled with light ice cream and other goodies, like fudge swirls or caramel. Seek out options with 150 calories or so and 5 grams of fat or less.

HG Trick! Can't find 'em and feeling super-sad about it? Don't panic; they couldn't be easier to make. Just let some light ice cream soften, stuff it inside a 50-calorie sugar cone along with a few mini semi-sweet chocolate chips, and freeze . . . Tada!

HG Heads-Up
The full-fat versions of these look very similar, and they are full of fat! There's no better way to tell than to just flip that box around and check the stats. And stick with brands known for diet-friendly stats.

HG Standouts: Weight Watchers and Skinny Cow.

Low-Fat Fudge Bars

These aren't quite as rich as full-on ice cream bars, but they tend to be lower in calories. There are small pops with about 50 calories each as well as larger 100-calorie bars.

HG Standouts: Weight Watchers Giant, Skinny Cow, Healthy Choice Premium, and No Sugar Added Fudgsicles.

HG Tip: Slide one off the stick and use it in chocolate-infused blended beverages . . . even COCKTAILS (if you're of the legal drinking age, of course)!

~ FRUITY OPTIONS ~

Fruit Bars

Fruit bars consist mostly of fruit with some added sugar. (Some have more sugar than others, so check stats if that's a concern.) They are typically fat-free with chunks of real fruit and come in flavors like lime and strawberry. Sweet and refreshing, these are a fun middle ground between snacking on apple slices and diving into a pint of ice cream. Look for bars with 130 calories or less. A summertime staple!

HG Heads-Up
Watch out for flavor names that include the word "cream." Those tend to contain fat—sometimes a LOT—and have higher calorie counts.

HG Standouts: Blue Bunny FrozFruit, Fruitfull, and Dreyer's/Edy's Fruit Bars.

Sorbet & Light Ice Cream Bars

These are the modern-day, grown-up version of Creamsicles—swirls of fruity sorbet and light vanilla ice cream, all situated on a stick for simple portion control. One of these has 100 calories or so and a gram or less of fat. And they come in berry varieties as well as classic orange. Score!

HG Standouts: Weight Watchers Giant Sorbet & Ice Cream Bars, Healthy Choice Premium Sorbet & Cream Bars, and No Sugar Added Creamsicles.

ICE CREAM & FROZEN DESSERTS

Sugar-Free Fruit-Flavored Ice Pops

How are these different from full-on fruit bars? They're not as substantial; they're usually half the size and much lower in calories. They're often made with artificial sweetener, while the bars are typically sweetened with sugar. Think of these as an incredibly low-calorie treat when you're craving something sweet and fruity. Look for skinny pops with about 15 calories each and larger ones with about 40 calories each—both should be fat-free.

> **HG Standout:** Sugar Free Popsicles.

~ OTHER DESSERT ITEMS ~ IN THE FREEZER

Mini Fillo Shells

No need to fuss with sheets of flaky fillo. These tiny shells are assembled and ready to go, and they have just about 15 calories each. Turn almost any food into hors d'oeuvres or mini desserts in a flash. Bake these shells according to the package instructions, and fill them with ANYTHING. Some dip or a bit of light cheese works like a charm for savory bites. Dollops of sugar-free pudding topped with fruit make for the easiest desserts around.

> **HG Standout:** Athens all the way . . .

Cool Whip Free

This frozen fat-free whipped topping in a tub is one amazing multi-tasker! It's a fantastic ingredient for recipes. To make pie-like fillings, custards, and mousse mixtures, just stir some CWF with equal parts sugar-free pudding. Or use it on its own as a creamy layer in desserts. It's also great frozen, as a straight ice cream swap. **(See the Ice Cream Swaparama on page 138 for proof!)** Cool Whip Free has 15 calories per 2-tablespoon serving. Wondering how it measures up against its refrigerated, in-a-can competitor, Fat Free Reddi-wip? Just see "Which One When?" on **page 15** to find out!

HG All-Star!
Vitalicious VitaTops

Everyone knows the best part of the muffin is the TOP. And VitaTops are, hands down, the BEST 100-calorie swap for cake, brownies, muffins, and more. Look for chocolate, corn, and fruity versions (or head online to vitalicious.com for the full lineup). These are all natural, high in fiber, and contain a few grams of protein. Yeah, WOW. There are so many ways to enjoy these, we could write an entire book on them alone. But for now, here are five fun ways . . .

* **Toasted and topped with low-sugar jam.** This method is perfect with the more breakfast-y flavors, like Golden Corn and BlueBran. So good! Slightly thaw before toasting for optimal results.

* **Broken or processed into crumbs, and used in layered desserts.** Whether in multi-serving trifles or single-serve parfaits, a layer of fluffy chocolate crumbles is amazing! Try this with fat-free yogurt, light ice cream, slightly sweetened fat-free cottage cheese, sugar-free pudding, and fruit. Just not all at once . . .

* **Freezy-Cool Whoopie Pies!** Carefully slice a frozen VitaTop into two round, thin pieces. Spoon a slightly softened serving of Cool Whip Free (or ¼ cup light vanilla ice cream) on top of one piece, and use the back of a spoon to spread it out evenly. Top it with the other Vita half, wrap it in plastic, and re-freeze 'til solid. Unreal!

* **With fruit.** Sounds simple but it's one of the best pairings EVER. A banana, a Fuji apple, or a bowl of berries alongside a VitaTop is probably the most satisfying way to spend around 200 calories.

* **With reduced-fat peanut butter and marshmallow creme.** Add either or both of these items to a chocolate Top for a Fluffernutter-like treat! Smear 'em on top or slice your Vita à la those Freezy-Cool Whoopie Pies.

ICE CREAM & FROZEN DESSERTS

Cake Cones and Sugar Cones

A small cake cone (that flat-bottomed one) has only 20 to 25 calories and less than a half-gram of fat. A small sugar one (pointy bottom) typically has 45 to 60 calories and a half-gram of fat or less—not bad either! Find these in the snack aisle, the baking section, or just outside the ice cream aisle.

HG Snack Ideas: You can fill these with other items besides ice cream. Spoon a pudding snack inside one and top with Fat Free Reddi-wip. Swirl some mini semi-sweet chocolate chips into light vanilla yogurt inside a cone. Or drizzle light chocolate syrup inside and freeze before filling. You can even bake lightened-up cupcakes inside the flat-bottomed cones.

HG Heads-Up
Beware of giant waffle and sugar cones. The larger the cone, the more calories and likelihood you'll fill it with several scoops of ice cream instead of just one!

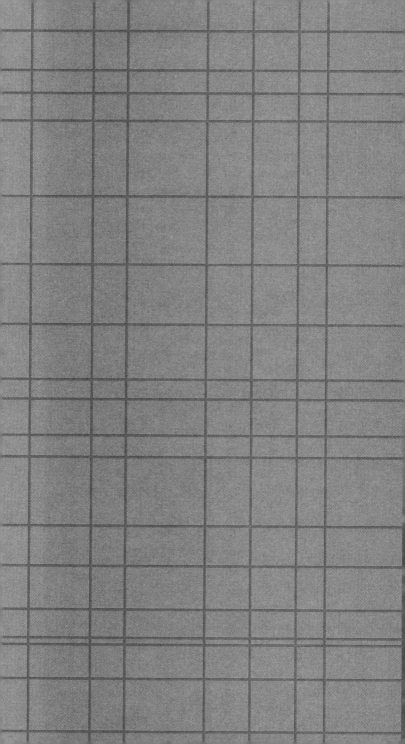

SAUCES, SALAD DRESSINGS, AND SHELF-STABLE CONDIMENTS

Light, Low-Fat, and Fat-Free Salad Dressings

There are many great-tasting options on shelves that have 25 to 60 calories and 5 grams of fat or less per 2-tablespoon serving. In addition to dressing your salads, use these in slaws, as veggie dips, as sandwich spreads, and even on top of grilled meats. Some HG favorites are low-fat sesame ginger dressing (see the All-Star on the next page!), fruity vinaigrettes (check calorie counts!), blue cheese (light or low-fat tastes better than fat-free), and honey mustard.

HG Tip: It's easy to overdo it when pouring dressing straight from the bottle onto your salad. (Restaurants often serve sides of dressing by the ½ cup . . . That's FOUR servings!) And those calories add up fast if you double or triple the serving size. So portion out a serving first, and consider using the dip-don't-pour method to make it go further.

HG Trick: Love the flavor of ranch but not crazy about the taste of the low-calorie versions? Try mixing some dry ranch dip/dressing mix into fat-free Greek yogurt or fat-free sour cream. You'll wind up with a flavorful, creamy concoction. Or mix the bottled dressing with some low-calorie BBQ sauce for a tangy take on ranch!

HG Standouts: Wish-Bone Light, Newman's Own Lighten Up!, Kraft Free, Kraft Light, low-calorie options from Litehouse, Hidden Valley Fat Free, and Girard's Fat Free.

HG Heads-Up

"Lite" doesn't always mean light. Sometimes it's just part of the brand name, so read labels carefully. Another important heads-up? Be wary of mom-n-pop brands of dressing with stats that seem too good to be true.

HG SHOCKER!

A common misconception is that all vinaigrettes are low in calories. We took a look at 33 vinaigrettes on shelves that weren't specifically labeled as light, and the average calorie and fat counts for a 2-tablespoon serving came to 102 calories and 10 grams of fat. ACK! The highest was a balsamic basil that tipped the scales with 170 calories and 17 grams of fat. Consider yourself warned.

Newman's Own Lighten Up! Low Fat Sesame Ginger Dressing

Words cannot express the incredibleness of this product. It's sweet and absolutely nothing about its taste says "guilt-free." It's also all natural and has just 35 calories and 1.5 grams of fat per 2-tablespoon serving. Toss it with broccoli cole slaw and chopped grilled chicken for a sassy Asian salad. Add it to wraps and drizzle it over steamed veggies. Or keep things classic and just enjoy it with a green salad!

Spray Dressings

This could be the invention of the century (or at least of 2006). Delicious guilt-free dressing is misted out of a spray bottle for optimal snack or meal coverage. A 10-spray serving has just 10 to 15 calories and 0.5 to 1 gram of fat. Top flavor picks include ranch, honey mustard, and Asian vinaigrettes. Best news? They're purse-friendly, so take 'em everywhere!

> **HG Standouts:** Wish-Bone Salad Spritzers and Ken's Lite Accents.

HG's TOP ATE Dressing Swaps

Check out these alternatives to the classic bottled dressing . . .

1. Salsa. Standard, fruity, southwest, or verde.
2. Fresh citrus juice. A squeeze of lemon, orange, or grapefruit juice is amazing over a plate of greens.
3. Marinade. Find a fat-free one, thin it out with a little water, and you're good to go!
4. Balsamic vinegar. Straight-up balsamic vinegar is sweet and packed with flavor.
5. Flavored mustard. If the consistency is too thick, add a little water or a squirt of citrus.
6. BBQ sauce. It's sweet, it's savory . . . Thin it out with a little H_2O.
7. Hot sauce. A few splashes are nice. Try mixing it with creamy dressing like ranch or blue cheese, too.
8. Seasoned rice vinegar. It's not just for cooking. Sweet and tangy . . . Yum!

Balsamic

This is the least vinegar-y of the vinegar family. It tastes like grape juice that's on its way to becoming a dessert wine. (This is a good thing.) In addition to topping salads with it, you can use it to punch up the flavor in tomato-based sauces, stir-frys, chilis, and stews. It's also amazing on grilled or steamed veggies. Some balsamics are thicker than others, which means more calories. Look for ones with about 10 calories per tablespoon.

BFF! Stir up a combo of balsamic vinegar and low-calorie BBQ sauce. Then use it anywhere you'd use either! BBQ-balsamic salad dressing? Sure! Balsamic-BBQ sauce on your chicken? Go for it!

Fun Find: Look for flavored balsamic vinegars like raspberry and fig. They're usually slightly higher in calories, around 25 per tablespoon, but they're so sweet and delicious you can use them as dessert toppings!

See page 199 for a secret online favorite!

Seasoned Rice Vinegar

Unlike standard rice vinegar (which is good, but less ready-to-use), this item has just enough salt and sugar added to it. It's the kind that's often served on cucumber salads (a.k.a. sunomono) at Japanese restaurants. And it's amazing over steamed spinach, thinly sliced chilled veggies, standard salads, and more. Use it in cole slaw and everyone will be asking for the recipe! A tablespoon of this has about 20 calories.

Apple Cider Vinegar, Red Wine Vinegar, and More

Apple cider vinegar is a key ingredient in homemade BBQ sauce (along with tomato sauce and brown sugar), and it's a great base for salad dressing if you're feeling crafty (try adding it to a mix of honey mustard and fat-free mayo). Red wine vinegar is another recipe staple for sauces, from sloppy joe to Asian-inspired dipping sauces.

What About Oil?

Unlike with cooking and baking, oil doesn't bring much to the table here. Check out the Baking Products section for more info on our oil preferences . . .

BBQ Sauce
with About 45 Calories Per Serving

Wondering why we didn't just call out "low-calorie BBQ sauce?" Because we don't want you to think you *have* to find a bottle that touts "Light!" or "Low Cal!!" You don't. The truth is that there are many BBQ sauces out there with 30 to 50 calories per 2-tablespoon serving. But there are just as many on shelves with 60 calories or more per 2-tablespoon serving. So browse around, peek at the labels, and find a favorite. Then use it on your favorite meats, seafood, veggies, and more. It's great slathered on top of a veggie patty, mixed with fat-free ranch dressing as a tangy dip, and combined with its BFF balsamic vinegar for a fun sauce or dressing.

HG Snack Idea: Craving slow-cooked, BBQ-style pulled chicken . . . minus the slow part? Shred up some cooked chicken and then top it with BBQ sauce that's been just slightly thinned out with water. Mix it up, heat it up, and eat it up!

BFF! You already know BBQ sauce is best buds with balsamic vinegar, but this sauce has another pal for life. Low-sugar or sugar-free fruit preserves! If fruity BBQ sounds good to you, try this out. Mix equal parts BBQ sauce with your fruit spread of choice (apricot's classic; raspberry's fun!), and you've got an amazing protein topper or stir-fry sauce!

> **HG Standouts:**
> Chris' & Pitt's and Stubb's.

Fat-Free Mayonnaise

Sure, fat-free mayo isn't the best-tasting stuff if you stick your spoon straight into the jar, but it's a great low-calorie base that's easy to doctor up. A tablespoon has just 10 calories. Add spices, herbs, and other low-calorie condiments like mustard, fat-free Greek yogurt, and hot sauce. And it's more than just a sandwich spread. Use it to whip up guilt-free scoopable salads like chicken salad and tuna salad. Create creamy sauces for fish or chicken. Throw together a DIY dip for veggies and more. Recent favorite add-ins? Chopped sun-dried tomatoes and garlic powder. YUM!

MAYO-A-MAYO
SEE HOW THEY STACK UP . . .

Regular mayo =
100 calories and 10 grams of fat per tablespoon

Light and reduced-fat mayo =
40 calories and 4 grams of fat per tablespoon

Fat-free mayo =
10 calories and <0.5 grams of fat per tablespoon

BOTTOM LINE: Standard mayo's a fat-tastrophe. Light and reduced-fat mayo are okay, if you only plan to spread a small amount on your sandwich. But fat-free mayo is essential, especially if you're likely to consume more than a single serving in one sitting.

HG All-Star!
Hellmann's/Best Foods Dijonnaise

Dijonnaise is, in a word, magical. It combines the richness of mayo with the subtle tanginess of mustard. You get yummy Dijon flavor with a little less "bite" than straight mustard. It's creamy and mild yet still has a lot of flavor. It's basically the perfect condiment (or at least in the top five!). And a teaspoon of it has just 5 fat-free calories. Use it nearly anywhere you'd use mayo or mustard. On sandwiches, burgers, and hot dogs, as well as in dips, scoopy salads, sauces, and slaws!

HG Trick: If your local store doesn't carry Dijonnaise (ah, the injustice!), try swirling some mild creamy Dijon mustard into fat-free mayo instead. It won't be exactly the same, but it'll still be pretty good!

Mustard

Honey, spicy brown, yellow, Dijon, deli-style . . . There are SO many mustards out there and most of them are SUPER low in calories. Honey mustards are higher than the others, with about 10 calories per teaspoon. The rest run around 5 calories per teaspoon. Get experimental and try out new stuff! Then use it to lend flavor to the blander things in life, like fat-free mayo and unadorned burger patties!

HG FYI:

Don't miss our TOP ATE Items Worth Ordering Online on page 199 for a sweet and mustard-y miracle condiment!

Ketchup

Heinz definitely makes the best-tasting ketchup. If you're watching your salt intake, try Heinz No Salt Added. Prefer things all natural? Check out Simply Heinz, sweetened with plain sugar. Do you go through so much ketchup per day that the typical 20-calories-per-tablespoon price tag is looking steep? Scoop up some 5-calorie, sucralose-sweetened Heinz Reduced Sugar. There's even Organic . . . Heinz has got you covered!

Hot Pepper Sauce

Spicy sauce is a great way to infuse your food with flavor for very few calories. Most hot sauces have 0 to 5 calories per teaspoon. Plus, spicy food can cause you to eat more slowly and fill up on less food—not a bad bonus! There are many styles and heat levels on shelves, from smoky to mild to super-fiery. Our pick? Buffalo-style! It makes everything taste like hot wings. Add it to skinless lean chicken, for starters. Then add that chicken to salads, wraps, pizzas, and more! It's also great on egg scrambles and stirred into soup.

HG Standouts: Hands down, Frank's RedHot Original Cayenne Pepper Sauce is number one. No contest. Tabasco has some unique options, as well.

Reduced-Fat Peanut Butter

There are many brands that make fat-slashed PB. On average, a 2-tablespoon serving has 190 calories, 12 grams of fat, and 2 grams of fiber. Looking for ways to stretch a portion? Mix it with a small amount of light vanilla soymilk to create a creamy PB sauce. Swirl it with marshmallow creme to cut the fat and add gooey-good marshmallow flavor. For a savory peanut butter sauce, mix with plain soymilk, fat-free yogurt, and spices. Whatever you do, don't just go at an open jar with a spoon!

HG Standouts: Skippy Reduced Fat Creamy and Reduced Fat Super Chunk, Jif Reduced Fat Creamy and Crunchy, and Peter Pan Whipped Creamy peanut butters. Another favorite? Justin's Nut Butters, even though those products aren't actually lower in fat. What they are is amazing in terms of taste and offered in portion-controlled packs. If your store carries 'em, snatch 'em up! If not, they're worth ordering online at justinsnutbutter.com.

HG Alternative: Looking for a way to get bits of peanut butter evenly distributed throughout your snack or dessert? Pick up peanut butter chips in the baking aisle. These cousins of chocolate chips contain around 80 calories and 4 grams of fat per tablespoon, and a single serving can go pretty far.

SAUCES, SALAD DRESSINGS, AND SHELF-STABLE CONDIMENTS

Better'n Peanut Butter/Peanut Wonder

The stuff has 40 percent fewer calories and a whopping 85 percent less fat than regular peanut butter, with just 100 calories and 2 grams of fat per 2-tablespoon serving. That is UNHEARD of! It's a little too sweet to pass as a straight-up peanut butter swap, but it's perfect for dessert recipes, smoothies, and snacks—try spreading it onto a giant chocolate rice cake! P.S. There's also a Low Sodium option.

> **The Where-to-Find 411:** This isn't a market staple across the globe, but more and more grocery stores are carrying it. If you don't see it with the other nut butters, check the diet or natural foods section.

Don't miss the TOP ATE Items Worth Ordering Online on page 199 for a super-special peanut butter find!

SAUCES, SALAD DRESSINGS, AND SHELF-STABLE CONDIMENTS

Sugar-Free and Low-Sugar Fruit Preserves and Jam

The sugar-free jellies taste great and have super-impressive stats, just 10 calories or so per tablespoon. But if you're willing to spend 25 calories per tablespoon, the low-sugar options from Smucker's taste RIDICULOUSLY good! All of these come in many, many flavors, so you'll never get bored! And check out our TOP ATE here . . .

> **HG Standouts:** Smucker's Sugar Free and Low Sugar Preserves and Jams, and Polaner Sugar Free Preserves with Fiber.

HG's TOP ATE
Uses for Sugar-Free and Low-Sugar Fruit Preserves and Jam!

1. As a base for sweet 'n savory glazes for chicken and veggies. Apricot works best here.

2. As a syrup-like dessert topping. Just warm it in the microwave with a little water, stir, and top away!

3. Stirred into fat-free yogurt (plain or vanilla; regular or Greek) or cottage cheese.

4. Spread onto toasted light bread, waffles, English muffins, pancakes, and more!

5. Swirled into oatmeal bowls . . . Mmmm!

6. As one half of a "hot couple" sauce—mix equal parts preserves and low-calorie BBQ sauce for a fruity grill-inspired sauce concoction!

7. The blackberry versions make a great stand-in when recipes like Swedish meatballs call for grape jelly. (SF grape jelly is so hard to find!)

8. With reduced-fat peanut butter! In any way, shape, or form . . .

Thick Marinades with 30 or Fewer Calories per Tablespoon

Teriyaki is probably the most common, but there are many other tasty marinades like spicy fruit flavors, Asian sesame, herby garlic, and southwest varieties. Look for options with 30 calories or less per tablespoon. The important thing to remember? Don't you dare limit these to meat marinating! Treat these as sauces or salad dressings. Top off burgers and sauce up your stir-frys. Use a marinade to coat cooked veggies. Thin one out for your new favorite salad dressing. Or spread some on your chicken, seafood, or protein of choice just prior to chomping in!

> **HG Standouts:** Lawry's, Newman's Own, and Mrs. Dash.

The Where-to-Find 411: You can find these in the Asian foods aisle, over by the salad dressings, or near the BBQ sauce setup.

Fat-Free Chicken, Beef, and Vegetable Gravy

This is one of those items that doesn't always announce itself as being free of fat. But flip around that jar and, surprise! A ¼-cup serving only has around 20 calories. A few brands have similar calorie counts with just 0.5 or 1 gram of fat per serving—also great! If you want to bump up the comfort-food feel of a meal, this is a good way to do it with little caloric consequence. Use it to make no-guilt shepherd's pie or egg foo young. Dip some faux-fried chicken strips in it. (See page 24 for the faux-frying 411!) Or just serve it with chicken 'n veggies for a homestyle, feel-good dinner!

Low-Fat Marinara, Pasta, and Pizza Sauce

Keep an eye on the fat content of your sauce! You might think, "How bad can tomato sauce be?" There are sauces that sneak in more oil, cheese, and added sugar than any tomato sauce needs, so ALWAYS check your labels. Look for options that top out at 70 calories and 3 grams of fat per ½-cup serving. And check the serving size, since some sauces list ¼ cup as the serving size.

Which One When?
Jarred Marinara, Pasta, or Pizza Sauce vs. Canned Crushed Tomatoes

When you're whipping up recipes with lots of decadent, flavor-packed, and potentially salty ingredients, there's no need to bring jarred sauce into the mix—canned crushed tomatoes bring just the right taste and texture for fewer calories, less fat, and (usually) less sodium. However, if you're trying to turn up the flavor on something somewhat basic—baked chicken, steamed veggies, or a low-fat egg scramble—the ready-to-go sauces are the way to go. And as a basic warm dip for assorted small bites, it's marinara or pizza sauce all the way.

Salsa

Chunks of tomatoes and other veggies seasoned up to perfection . . . What could be better? Don't just stick to standard jarred varieties either. Look for fruity tomato-based salsa, like peach and pineapple. (Or DIY—see our list of TOP ATE Types of Fruit to Add to Salsa on page 74!) Southwest-style salsa, with black beans and corn, is super-delicious (but slightly higher in calories). Salsa verde has a mild flavor that's all its own. And check out the fresh salsa packed in tubs in the refrigerated sections—these tend to be a little pricier, but worth it. Basic salsas have about 10 to 20 calories per 2-tablespoon serving and are virtually fat-free.

HG Tip: Salsa is an INCREDIBLE shortcut ingredient, especially if you're cooking for one; instead of chopping up a ridiculously small amount of tomatoes, peppers, onions, etc., a spoonful or two of salsa will help boost the flavor of your single-serving meal.

HG Snack Ideas: Dip cut veggies (like bell pepper strips and jicama sticks) into salsa for a crazy-low-calorie, crunchy snack. Use salsa as a topping for baked fish or chicken. Mix it with canned or pouched albacore tuna for a speedy, protein-packed snack—great on rice cakes or high-fiber crackers. Use it as a dip for steamed artichoke leaves. You can even use it as a dressing alternative on your salad greens. It's also the easiest way to bring Mexican flavor to anything you're eating (cupcakes excluded).

Salt-Slashing 411: If the salt content of the salsa on shelves is an issue, you have a few options. Seek out salt-free or low-sodium varieties. (These are more often in the fridge section.) Ditch the pre-made kind altogether and do it yourself by mixing diced tomato, onion, peppers, spices, and herbs. Try canned fire-roasted tomatoes as a lower-sodium salsa option. Or, our favorite, the happy medium: Mix jarred salsa with diced tomato (fresh or canned with little to no salt) for a lot less sodium without too much work.

> More tomato sauce options await you in the Canned Foods section!

SAUCES, SALAD DRESSINGS, AND SHELF-STABLE CONDIMENTS

Reduced-Sodium/Lite Soy Sauce

No, lite soy sauce isn't an implication that other soy sauce is fatty; it just means this type has about ⅓ʳᵈ less sodium than the regular kind. This salty, savory, classic Asian condiment has about 10 calories per tablespoon. It's a staple ingredient for creating Chinese-style food at home. Even if you don't want to go all out with a recipe, steamed veggies and plain chicken seem a whole lot more interesting with a splash of soy. If you do want to get a little crazy in the kitchen, try pairing soy sauce with sweeter condiments like seasoned rice vinegar and juice from canned fruit—stir in a little cornstarch, and you're on your way to sweet 'n sour something!

Sweet Asian Chili Sauce

A teaspoon of this sweet and sticky stuff has around 10 fat-free calories. But since it is on the dense side, an over-pour can cause calories to add up fast. Use it sparingly and make it go further by mixing it with sauces and condiments like fat-free mayo, canned tomato sauce, and seasoned rice vinegar. Then use it on seafood, in noodle dishes, with chicken, and on veggies. Yum!

> Don't miss more Asian products in the Canned Foods and Baking Products sections!

SAUCES, SALAD DRESSINGS, AND SHELF-STABLE CONDIMENTS

Taco Sauce

This tomato-based sauce usually comes in a bottle, is red (green is rare), and has 5 to 10 calories per tablespoon. It's pretty thick and packed with intense Mexican flavors like chile, onion, and garlic. Look for mild, medium, and spicy, and choose your comfort level. Use this sauce to infuse foods with lots of flavor without adding a lot of calories (or liquid)—things like shredded chicken, ground meat, and saucy fillings for burritos and more. Or just add a little to anything that needs a concentrated POP of Mexican flavor.

Enchilada Sauce

This sauce is available in both red and green, can be found in either cans or jars, and has around 20 calories per ¼-cup serving. It's almost like a smooth version of salsa, and the green kind has a really nice, mild, almost sweet flavor. Great for smothering tortilla-wrapped goodies like enchiladas, burritos, and taquitos (especially those with corn tortillas!), and it also works well as a dipping sauce. It's even found its way into an HG soup recipe or two, where it tastes fantastic!

Sugar-Free Pancake Syrup

Sugar-free pancake syrup, which has around 30 calories per
¼-cup serving, is sweet, sticky, and all-around delicious. Use
it with low-fat waffles and pancakes as well as guilt-free French
toast. (There's an entire chapter of French toast recipes in *Hungry
Girl 1-2-3: The Easiest, Most Delicious, Guilt-Free Recipes
on the Planet!*) It's also a great ingredient for sweet sauces and
baked goods; it adds sweetness, velvety texture, and maple-y
flavor while keeping sugary calories to a minimum.

HG Standouts: Cary's Sugar Free,
Mrs. Butterworth's Sugar Free, and Log Cabin
Sugar Free.

PANCAKE SYRUP SHOWDOWN

*What are the different calorie counts for an average ¼-cup
serving of the common types of pancake syrup?*

Regular/original/100% maple syrup = 200 calories

Lite/light/reduced-calorie syrup = 100 calories

Sugar-free/low-calorie syrup = 30 calories

BOTTOM LINE: A ¼-cup serving might sound like a
lot of syrup, but it's actually a realistic amount for pancake,
waffle, and French toast topping 'n dipping. And while regular
maple syrup is unsurprisingly high in calories, the difference
between lite and sugar-free syrup is massive! Use the lite
kind sparingly if you want to infuse recipes with maple-y
sweetness without any artificial sweetener. But as a staple
breakfast condiment that won't cause calorie counts in your
morning meals to skyrocket, sugar-free pancake syrup is
your best bet.

SAUCES, SALAD DRESSINGS, AND
SHELF-STABLE CONDIMENTS

Jet-Puffed Marshmallow Creme

This marshmallow goo makes a terrific base for guilt-free glazes, frostings, and icings. It's also great, as is, for topping off ice cream. The flavor and texture are perfect; sweet, airy, fluffy, and fantastic. And the stats can't be beat: just 20 calories per tablespoon!

HG Snack Ideas: Grab some caramel-flavored soy crisps or mini rice cakes, and top them off with a spoonful of creme. Then pop 'em right into your mouth or serve them sandwich-style, one on top of the other! This works with other sweet soy crisps and rice cakes, as well as low-fat graham crackers! Another fun use? As a dip for fresh fruit. Yes!

HG Tricks: If your marshmallow creme has been in the pantry for a while and is not as fluffy as it once was, try microwaving it before you mix it into a recipe. To keep it from sticking to your measuring cups and spoons, spray your utensils with a little nonstick cooking spray. And for a more drizzlable marshmallow topping, add a bit of light vanilla soymilk, and then warm it in the microwave and stir until smooth.

Light and Fat-Free Caramel Dip

These two are basically interchangeable without affecting the stats of your snack or dessert very much at all. A 2-tablespoon serving of the light kind contains about 100 calories and 1.5 grams of fat. The fat-free dip has 110 to 120 calories. And since you'll rarely consume a full serving in one sitting (in most cases, a ½ tablespoon is enough) the difference really is negligible. Now that the numbers are out of the way, check out our TOP ATE uses for the sweet, gooey goodness on the next page!

HG Tip: Sometimes the regular and original versions of caramel dip have stats similar to these. So if you don't see a clearly labeled light option, check nutritional panels for an acceptable dip.

HG Standouts: Marzetti Light and Fat Free Caramel Dip, and Litehouse Low Fat and Original.

The Where-to-Find 411: Look for these shelf-stable tubs in the produce section. Why produce? Because they're often positioned as apple dips. And now you know . . .

Light and Sugar-Free Chocolate Syrup

Even if you don't make ice cream sundaes all that often, chocolate syrup can come in handy. (See the TOP ATE list below for proof!) It can help amp up the chocolate flavor in lightened-up baked desserts—just add it to the batter. The light syrup has about 50 calories per 2-tablespoon serving and a nice rich flavor. The sugar-free kind is a major calorie bargain, with just 15 calories per 2-tablespoon serving. It isn't quite as decadent in taste as light chocolate syrup, but it's a great way to keep calories in check when your dessert or drink of choice is already pretty indulgent.

HG Heads-Up

Some sugar-free syrups have a fake-ish flavor and bitter aftertaste. Stick to brands you know and love, and avoid the others.

HG Standouts: Hershey's Lite and Sugar Free syrups. HANDS DOWN. The brilliant minds at Hershey's even recently improved their formulas, making these sweet syrups taste even better.

HG Snack Idea: Slice a banana in half and stab a Popsicle stick through the cut end. Douse it in syrup and, if you like, sprinkle with a small amount of crushed nuts or sprinkles. Then freeze it for a super-fun, guilt-free treat!

HG's TOP ATE Uses for
Light and Fat-Free Caramel Dip AND
Light and Sugar-Free Chocolate Syrup

1. As a stir-in addition to coffee, hot cocoa, and other hot drinks.

2. Squiggled over fruity parfaits, light yogurt (especially caramel dip in Greek yogurt), sugar-free pudding, and light ice cream!

3. As a dip or topping for apple slices, banana coins, pear halves, peach chunks, and [your favorite fruit here]!

4. Added to cottage cheese and oatmeal for a dessert-like twist on breakfast!

5. As a schmancy topping on low-fat waffles and pancakes.

6. When making super-simple dessert dips with Cool Whip Free, sugar-free pudding, light yogurt, and fat-free or low-fat ricotta cheese.

7. In blended beverages, from "swappuccinos" to smoothies and shakes!

8. Two words: Cupcake. Topping.

SAUCES, SALAD DRESSINGS, AND SHELF-STABLE CONDIMENTS

BEVERAGES

Calorie-Free
Less than 5 calories per serving.

Low-Calorie
40 calories or less per serving.

Light/Lite
At least 33 percent fewer calories than the standard version.

Reduced-Calorie/Less Calories
At least 25 percent fewer calories than the standard version.

"Diet"
Usually used in combination with one of the claims above. In other words? Read the fine print to see which of the above applies.

~ WATER ~

BEVERAGES

Flavored Water

Straight-up H_2O is the purest way to hydrate. But if you have trouble getting in your daily eight glasses, flavored waters can help. These run the gamut from lightly flavored with only fruit essence to fully flavored and sweetened. The standouts below are listed from the most mild to the boldest. Seek out sips with no more than 20 calories per serving, and check the labels for the total servings per bottle.

HG Standouts: Aquafina FlavorSplash, Zero-Calorie SoBe Lifewater, Vitaminwater Zero, and Activate Drinks.

HG Heads-Up
Just because something has the word "water" in the name, doesn't mean it's low in calories. Some flavored waters are loaded with sugar and have as many calories as soda. OUCH! Check those labels . . .

Kid-Targeted Beverage Finds: If the idea of stabbing a shiny pouch of liquid with a small straw excites you, check out Minute Maid Fruit Falls and Just 10 Pouches. Low in calories (5 to 10 each) and super-delicious!

HG Trick: Enjoy lightly flavored water but want to DIY? Just add a few fruit slices (apple, orange, lemon, or lime) to a pitcher, and fill 'er up with H_2O. Or try cucumber slices for a schmancy spa-like sipper. Fun, fun, fun!

Coconut Water

Pure coconut water, the clear liquid from inside the coconut, is getting a lot of buzz these days. And although we're pretty selective when it comes to caloric beverages, this stuff has incredible health benefits and tastes amazing! It has tons of potassium and electrolytes, and some experts say it hydrates better than regular water. Plus, the stats are pretty reasonable: 1 cup has about 45 calories and less than 1 gram of fat. There are also fruity flavors out there with similar stats. A great addition to your beverage rotation!

> **HG Standouts:** Zico, O.N.E., and Vita Coco.

HG Heads-Up
Always read labels carefully; watch out for added sugar and extra calories.

HG SHOCKER!

Whatever you do, don't confuse coconut *milk* with coconut water. Coconut milk—the thick, creamy, canned ingredient that's made from a concentrated amount of coconut meat—contains more than 450 calories and 50 grams of fat per cup! Even the "lite" kind has at least a dozen fat grams per cup. So don't confuse the two! Got it? Good!

For a creamy coconut drink, flip to page 19 for the 411 on light coconut milk beverages . . . They don't come in cans and they won't obliterate your diet!

Spring Water

If your tap water's not palatable, you've got a few options. Drink it anyway (kidding!), pick up a faucet filter (the most eco-friendly solution), or stock up on spring water! Stores stock everything from 8-ounce mini bottles to massive jugs. So grab whatever suits your needs. P.S. Spring water is calorie-free. (Yay!)

HG Tip: Treat yourself to a cute refillable water bottle. Then fill it with your water of choice, and go to town! (Literally. That's one of the benefits of the bottle's portability.)

Light Juice Beverages

You probably know that whole fruit is more satisfying than a cup of juice. But sometimes, you just really want a glass of OJ! Or AJ! Or the juice of some other fruit! But since regular juice carries a pretty high calorie price tag of 100+ calories per 8-ounce serving, it's nice to know there are light options. Look for those with 50 or fewer calories per cup. The standouts outlined below taste PHENOMENAL!

> **HG Standouts:** Trop50, V8 V-Fusion Light, and Ocean Spray Light.

Low-Calorie Juice Drinks

Often called "diet," low-calorie juice drinks are a little less juice-like than the light beverages above. But these drinks are a great way to get a sweet, fruity fix for very few calories. Seek out options with 20 or fewer calories per 8-ounce serving.

> **HG Standouts:** Ocean Spray Diet, and Diet V8 Splash (especially the Tropical Blend!).

HG Tip: There's a fine line between flavored watered and low-calorie juice drinks these days. So hop on over to the Water section on **page 168** for a few more fruity options!

Fun Uses for Light and Low-Calorie Juice Drinks!

* Mix some 50/50 with diet soda for a fizzy, fruity free-for-all!
* Use them as mixers for guilt-free cocktails.
* Blend with other guilt-free ingredients for a smoothie or slushie!
* Enjoy a serving over many crushed ice cubes with a bendy straw. Because crushed ice is awesome, and everything tastes better out of a bendy straw . . .

Sugar-Free Powdered Drink Mixes

Sticks of low-calorie drink mix are great when you're on the go and need a fruity beverage fix. The packets are convenient since they can easily be stashed in your purse or pocket. In addition to fruit flavors, there are iced tea options that rock. These are great for making cocktails and mocktails. (Just be careful, because the intense sweetness can make alcohol seem less potent than it is.) Sugar-free powdered drink mixes typically have 5 calories per serving, which is actually half a packet in most cases. Why half a packet? Because each packet makes two 8-ounce servings. (But really, most people use one packet at a time.)

> **HG Standouts:** Crystal Light, Wyler's Light, Lipton Iced Tea To Go, and AriZona Sugar Free.

HG All-Natural Picks: True Lemonade and Crystal Light Pure.

* NEED-TO-KNOW LINGO *
NO-CALORIE SWEETENER IN DRINKS EDITION

Aspartame

Low-calorie artificial sweetener that's been around for a couple of decades and used in tons of food and drink products.

Aliases: NutraSweet, Equal
Found In: Coke Zero (and fellow Zero products), Crystal Light, Lipton Iced Tea To Go

Stevia

The sweetener du jour is made from the naturally sweet leaves of the stevia plant.

Aliases: Truvia, Pure Via, Reb A
Found In: Trop50, Vitaminwater Zero, Zero-Calorie SoBe Lifewater, Activate Drinks, True Lemonade

Sucralose

Among artificial sweeteners, it's the sweetest, which means a small amount is all it takes. And arguably, it's the type that tastes most like real sugar.

Alias: Splenda
Found In: Ocean Spray Diet, Diet V8 Splash, AriZona Diet and Sugar Free, Aquafina FlavorSplash

See page 191 for more on no-calorie sweeteners.

Diet Soda and Club Soda

Sometimes, you may feel like you REALLY want a soda. And as far
as vices go, the occasional cup of calorie-free cola isn't all that bad.
For a fun spin on an ice cream float, pour your favorite soda flavor
into a chilled mug, and top it off with a scoop of frozen Cool Whip Free.
Or go all out and add light ice cream instead!

> **HG Standouts:** Coke Zero, Coke Cherry Zero,
> Sprite Zero, A&W Diet Root Beer, and Dr. Brown's Diet.

HG All-Natural Picks: Stevia-sweetened sodas are
definitely not yet a market staple. And many brands have a funny,
"off" taste. But a real winner in our book? Blue Sky Free! Great
flavor options, fantastic taste, no calories. The Creamy Root Beer
is the best. Woohoo!

HG SHOCKER!

> Think tonic water is the same as zero-calorie club soda?
> It SO isn't. It has almost as many calories as regular
> soda—about 100 per cup! Stick to club soda or locate
> some diet tonic . . .

> See the cake mix section on page 182 for a diet-soda surprise!

BEVERAGES

Diet Iced Tea

Chilly tea can be deliciously refreshing. And it's even better when someone else has brewed it for you. Look for teas with 10 calories or less per 8-ounce serving. Wanna couple up this drink with another on the list? Mix it with light or sugar-free lemonade for a low-calorie Arnold Palmer. So good!

HG Standouts: Diet Snapple and Diet AriZona.

* NEED-TO-KNOW LINGO *
SUGAR EDITION

Sugar-Free
Less than 0.5 grams of sugar per serving.

Reduced-Sugar/Less Sugar
At least 25 percent less sugar than the standard version.

No Added Sugars
No sugar or sugar-containing ingredient has been added during processing. (Naturally occurring sugars are fair game.)

Unsweetened Iced Tea

There are many brewed unsweetened teas on shelves these days. Just add lemon and your sweetener of choice, and you're done!

HG Standouts: Tejava and Gold Peak Tea.

Ready-to-Brew Coffee

Coffee beans themselves are virtually calorie-free, so just monitor those add-ins. Go for ground, whole bean, or those little containers made for single-cup brewers (K-Cups rock our socks!). **See page 203** for our ultimate Coffee Drink Essentials list!

> **HG Standouts:** Millstone, Green Mountain, and Dunkin' Donuts.

Instant Coffee

This stuff is super-convenient, and it tastes better than you think. Obviously, it's ideal for super-speedy hot coffee cups. But it's even more helpful for making iced or blended coffee-based drinks! Use it to infuse mocha flavor into chocolatey treats. (First dissolve it in a little water; don't just add the granules to pudding cups!) Check out the Coffee Drink Essentials list on **page 203** for all your coffee-making needs!

> **HG Standouts:** Folgers, Nescafé Taster's Choice, and our All-Star below!

HG All-Star!
Starbucks VIA Ready Brew

This is the best instant coffee EVER! The individual packets aren't cheap, but they are less expensive than buying daily cups from Starbucks. Stick with the regular roasts if you want to keep things basically calorie-free. The flavored varieties are sugar-sweetened and contain 60 calories. Not bad for a super-convenient flavored coffee fix!

BEVERAGES

Hot Cocoa Packets with 20 to 25 Calories Each

These are crazy-low in calories yet completely rich and delicious. If you wanna whip up something really special, ignore the 6-ounce cup suggestion. (Too small!) Add a bit more water and toss in some other things as well: cocoa powder, no-calorie sweetener, flavored extract (yay, coconut!), fat-free or sugar-free powdered creamer, and more. All amazing. ENJOY!!!

> **Recipe Ideas:** These packets have fantastic chocolate-boosting abilities—just dissolve one in a small amount of water, and then mix it into dessert batters, smoothies, coffee drinks . . . even oatmeal!

> **HG Standouts:** Swiss Miss Diet and Nestlé Fat Free.

Tea Bags

There's a tea out there for pretty much any flavor craving. Fruity green tea, spicy chai tea, herby hibiscus tea . . . You name it, they make it. Hot tea is a fantastic way to keep from diving into the snack closet when you know you're not *really* hungry (just bored, tired, or some other emotion easily confused with hunger). It's also soothing and all-around enjoyable. And if you're patient enough to brew up a few bags, add cold water, and let it chill completely in the fridge, you can have iced tea in whatever flavor and with whatever sweetener you could possibly want.

> **HG Tip:** Check out the seasonal options that pop up during the holidays. Candy cane and sugar cookie?! Awesome.

> **HG Standouts:** Celestial Seasonings, Tazo, and Stash.

Unsweetened Instant Iced Tea Mix

This is like the tea version of instant coffee. It may be old-school, but it's HANDY! If you want a glass of iced tea, but don't want to go through the whole steeping/chilling/icing hullabaloo, adding this to water is a simple and calorie-free way to get iced tea in no time flat. And if you want to mix your own juice-tea blend, this will help out big-time.

---

* Don't miss the Coffee Drink Essentials on page 203!
* Do NOT miss Unsweetened Vanilla Almond Breeze, light vanilla soymilk, and more in the Dairy section!

BAKING PRODUCTS, PANTRY STAPLES, SPICES, AND MORE

Whole-Wheat Flour

Whether wheat or white, flour is calorie-dense. A ¼-cup serving of either kind has about 110 calories. Best bets? Look for flour labeled "whole-wheat" or "whole grain"—not just "wheat"—with about 4 grams of fiber per ¼ cup. We think this better-for-you flour tastes great in recipes and is a totally reasonable swap for the white stuff.

HG Trick! When working with sticky dough **(like the kinds outlined on page 122)**, a sprinkling of flour on your rolling pin and work surface will make the process so much easier! And it'll only add a scant amount of calories.

Cornmeal

This grainy grind is definitely underrated. Add a little to the breadcrumb coating of your "faux-fried" goodies for extra flavor! **(Find the faux-frying 411 on page 24.)** A ¼-cup serving contains about 125 calories and 2.5 grams of fiber.

Pancake Mix

This is a great item to keep on hand for days when you don't feel like following a full-on recipe. But don't just follow the box directions if they suggest adding things like whole eggs, oil, and full-fat milk! Swap these things out for fat-free liquid egg substitute, canned pumpkin or no-sugar-added applesauce, and light vanilla soymilk or another light milk swap. Look for mixes that are low in fat with about 150 calories per ⅓-cup serving. Serving sizes vary with these, so look for a calorie count of about 120 if the serving size is ¼ cup. Bonus points if it packs fiber!

> **HG Standouts:** Aunt Jemima Whole Wheat Blend Pancake & Waffle Mix, Hungry Jack Complete Extra Light & Fluffy, Fiber One Complete Pancake Mix, and Bisquick Heart Smart Pancake and Baking Mix.

Cornstarch

Great for thickening broths into sauces! Whisk into cold liquid and then cook—it's so basic, but it never ceases to amaze. A tablespoon has 30 calories and does the trick.

Baking Powder

Not the same as baking soda! Baking powder is actually baking soda plus an added element that activates the baking soda. Convenient! Baking powder helps make your baked goods fluffier. Don't go overboard with the stuff though, or your food might taste salty! P.S. It's pretty much calorie-free.

Mini Semi-Sweet Chocolate Chips

Why miniature chips? For one thing, they're easier to measure in small amounts. (Try putting regular-sized chocolate chips into a teaspoon—you'll get a few chips in there and a lot of empty space!) Portion control and accuracy are important when you're dealing with something like pure chocolate! Another reason minis rock? Those little bits distribute themselves really well, so you can use less than you'd need with larger pieces. Each 1-tablespoon serving has about 75 calories and 4 grams of fat.

> **HG Snack Ideas:** Stir a teaspoon into a sugar-free vanilla pudding snack, a container of fat-free yogurt . . . even oatmeal or fat-free cottage cheese. You'll get an infusion of chocolatey goodness for around 25 calories and 1.25 grams of fat!

Peanut Butter Chips

These are the creamy, peanut butter version of chocolate chips. In fact, the stats are nearly the same—a 1-tablespoon serving has about 80 calories and 4 grams of fat. These are a terrific way to add a bit of PB flavor to foods without getting into a sticky situation with the real deal. And by sticky situation, we're referring to the likelihood of eating several spoonfuls straight from the jar. Crush or chop these up to really stretch a serving!

For more peanut butter picks, see page 155.

Mini Marshmallows

With these you can take something ordinary and make it much cooler. A cup of hot cocoa, a scoop of light ice cream, and (of course!) anything s'mores inspired. Mini 'mallows are fat-free, and a ⅔-cup serving has around 100 calories. That's about 45 mini marshmallows, by the way. (We counted.)

HG FYI:

Jet-Puffed Marshmallow Creme is another great way to enjoy the classic treat known as marshmallow. See page 164 for the 411.

Don't miss the DIY 100-Calorie Packs mini guide on page 111. Then make portion-controlled treats with chocolate chips, marshmallows, and more!

Shredded Sweetened Coconut

With high-fat foods, small pieces work so well in recipes and snack assembly. A small spoonful of these flakes will go far in oatmeal bowls, fruit parfaits, and guilt-free dessert recipes. On average, a tablespoon of the sweetened shreds has 30 calories and 3 grams of fat.

HG Trick! Toasting coconut is incredibly simple—just put shreds in a dry skillet, and cook over medium heat on the stove until toasty. Easy and delicious!

Chocolate and Rainbow Sprinkles

Good news: Sprinkles have only about 20 calories and 1 gram of fat per teaspoon, which is nice because you rarely ever need more than that. These are fun, plain and simple. Use them to top off light ice cream and low-fat cupcakes.

HG Snack Idea: Make a frozen waffle or pancake feel really special. Warm it up and top with a serving of Fat Free Reddi-wip, a teaspoon of sprinkles, and a drizzle of light chocolate syrup. Sure, it's a little junk-food-y, but it's a lot lower in calories than similar stuff served at waffle and pancake houses!

Unsweetened Cocoa Powder

Cocoa powder adds chocolate flavor for a small amount of fat and very few calories. It isn't sweet but it boosts the chocolate taste in whatever you add it to. A whole tablespoon has only 12 calories and less than a gram of fat! Great for baking, making at-home mochas, creating cocoa-infused oatmeal, and more. Plus, a canister will last a very long time.

BAKING PRODUCTS, PANTRY STAPLES, SPICES, AND MORE

Moist-Style Cake Mixes

The most important thing to know about cake mix? You don't need to follow the instructions on the box. Most recommend adding eggs and oil, but there's just no need for all that added fat and calories. Check out the two-ingredient cake ideas below. In terms of the kind of mix you buy, moist-style cake mixes are the best because MOIST CAKE ROCKS! The stats on cake mix are all pretty similar—about 170 calories and 3.5 grams of fat per serving ($\frac{1}{12}$th of the mix itself). Reduced-sugar mixes like the kind by Pillsbury have about half as much sugar as regular mixes. The calorie counts are only slightly lower though.

Two-Ingredient Cake ... THREE Ways!

Grab an 18.25-ounce box of cake mix, and choose one of the options below. As difficult as it might be, IGNORE any and all additional ingredients the directions on the box might mention. Follow the oven temp. and time instructions on the box, and you'll have cake with about 180 calories and 3.5 grams of fat per serving ($\frac{1}{12}$th of cake). This saves you lots of calories and fat!

No-Sugar-Added Applesauce — This works best with yellow cake mix. Add **1 cup of applesauce**, and you'll end up with a moist and fluffy cake that's sweet and has a slight apple flavor.

Diet Soda — While great with any cake and soda combo, yellow cake mix and diet cream soda are one amazing duo. Use a **12-ounce can of the soda** for a tasty treat that's REALLY impressive!

Canned Pure Pumpkin — Grab a **15-ounce can of pure pumpkin** and a box of devil's food cake mix. Bake at 400 degrees for brownie-like treats!

BAKING PRODUCTS, PANTRY STAPLES, SPICES, AND MORE

Brownie Mix

Surprisingly, most brownie mix is low in fat. A serving of the mix itself has about 110 calories and 2 grams of fat. But as with cake mix, the trick is to avoid adding all the butter, eggs, and oil that are typically called for. Our favorite way to use brownie mix? To make fudge. Just mix an 18.3-ounce box with 2 cups of canned pumpkin, and bake for 35 minutes or so at 350 degrees. Let it chill completely, uncovered, in the fridge. Then cut into 36 squares and chew! Just 60 calories or so per square.

> **HG Standout:** No Pudge! Fat Free Fudge Brownie Mix. The box actually gives you guilt-free instructions! A little fat-free yogurt and you're on your way to brownie town. There's even a single-serving recipe, for those of us who can't be trusted with a whole pan of brownies. A serving of the mix itself has 110 calories.

HG Trick: That single-serving recipe just mentioned? We're spilling the details so you can make it with any mix! Combine 2 tablespoons of brownie mix with 1 tablespoon of fat-free vanilla yogurt. Stir until smooth, and microwave for a minute. Tada!

> For an amazing brownie-like swap located in the freezer aisle, check out chocolate-flavored Vitalicious VitaTops!

Frosting Swaparama and Super-Sizing!

Canned frosting has an alarming average of 120 calories and 5 fat grams per 2-tablespoon serving. Here are some tips and tricks for topping off your baked goods . . .

Sugar-Free Pudding — Pre-made pudding snacks are perfect when mixed with a little real frosting. Great gooey texture; great way to stretch a frosting serving.

Cool Whip Free — On its own or blended with other items on this list, this is a nice light topping for cupcakes and more.

Jet-Puffed Marshmallow Creme — A great ingredient to mix with whipped topping. Make sure it's soft and fresh for easy stirring.

Fat-Free or Reduced-Fat Cream Cheese — Okay, clearly not a swap by itself, but mixed with whipped topping, marshmallow creme, and a bit of extra sweetener, you can make a great guilt-free cream cheese frosting!

Light or Fat-Free Caramel Dip — Combine it with sugar-free pudding and shredded coconut, and you've got faux German chocolate frosting. Mmmm!

Low-Fat Graham Crackers and Chocolate Graham Crackers

More cookie-ish than cracker-y, grahams are fantastic. They're sweet, but not overwhelmingly so, and crunchy. And they give you quite the bang for your calorie buck. Each sheet (that's 4 crackers) of low-fat grahams has around 60 calories and 1 gram of fat. Those come in honey and cinnamon flavors. The standard chocolate ones are great too—a sheet has 70 calories or so and 2 grams of fat. Check out the TOP ATE list below for some great snack ideas!

HG's TOP ATE
Uses for Graham Crackers

1. Break a sheet in half and make a frozen ice cream sandwich, using real light ice cream or Cool Whip Free!

2. Indoor s'mores! Keep portions in check with mini chocolate chips and marshmallows.

3. Grind them up in a blender with Fiber One Original cereal. Mix with melted light butter and press into a pie pan. Bake and let cool for a sweet high-fiber pie crust! See page 24 for specifics.

4. Break chocolate ones into pieces, and stir or blend into light vanilla ice cream shakes. It's like an Oreo shake! (Use light vanilla soymilk and lots of crushed ice too.)

5. Those pie-flavored fat-free yogurt cups? Top with crushed grahams for an instant upside-down pie fix! (Sugar-free pudding snacks also work well.)

6. Make dessert sandwiches with things like fruit preserves, marshmallow creme, reduced-fat PB, and banana slices!

7. Crush 'em up and use as a granola swap in fruit 'n yogurt parfaits.

8. Top a mug of hot cocoa with marshmallows and crushed grahams. S'mores hot chocolate!

Sugar-Free Fat-Free Instant Pudding Mix

Jell-O's boxed mixes taste the best. Hands-down. ESPECIALLY when it comes to vanilla. With that out of the way, instant pudding mix (in all flavors!) rocks. And the stats on the sugar-free, fat-free kinds are super-impressive: A serving of the mix itself has just about 30 calories. Prepared with fat-free milk, that's about 80 calories per ½-cup serving. Nice!

HG Heads-Up
Instant pudding will NOT set if mixed with soymilk, almond milk, or anything other than real dairy milk. So use fat-free dairy milk when you make instant pudding.

> **HG Standout:** Jell-O Sugar Free Fat Free Instant.

HG Trick: Did you know that sugar-free dry pudding mix makes a TERRIFIC ingredient when making guilt-free shakes or eggless nog? IT DOES! It thickens your drinks and makes them extra creamy!

Nonstick Cooking Spray

Nonstick spray is essential for whipping up guilt-free items. Use it when you make omelettes, stir-frys, pancakes, and pretty much anything else you'd prepare stovetop in a skillet. When baking, it'll keep cakes, cupcakes, meatloaf, chicken, anything, and everything from sticking. When it comes to the zero-calorie and fat-free claims, here's what you NEED to know. While there are zero calories and fat grams in a single serving, a typical serving size is a "¼-second spray." There are actually about 5 to 10 calories and 0.5 gram to 1 gram of fat in a (more realistic) 1-second spray. Still MUCH less than what you'd be taking in if you used regular cooking oil! The problem, though, is that some people think nonstick cooking spray is absolutely calorie-free and fat-free and drench their baking sheets, skillets, and pans with the stuff. Try not to fall into that trap. Stick with the spray, but don't go crazy with it.

> **HG Standouts:** Pam Original, Professional High Heat, Olive Oil, and Butter Flavor.

HG SHOCKER!

There are about 500 quarter-second servings in a standard can of cooking spray. At 7 calories per 1-second spray, that's nearly 900 calories in that can! Food for thought if you find yourself going through a can quickly . . .

If there are only trace amounts of calories (less than 5) and fat (less than 0.5 grams) in the given serving, a company is allowed to say its product has zero calories and is fat-free. This means each serving of a calorie-free, fat-free food can have up to 4 calories and 0.4 grams of fat.

Bottom Line: Pay attention to portion sizes! If you're consuming many servings of something and questioning its impact on your daily fat and calories, these hidden calories and fat grams could be to blame.

Olive Oil

From a fat and calorie standpoint, oil is oil. Vegetable, canola, olive, etc., all have about 120 calories and 14 grams of fat per tablespoon. That adds up quickly. For baking and stovetop cooking, stick with the sprays to keep amounts at a minimum. But there is a time and place for real olive oil. Use it to bring out rich flavor in veggies. They're already low in calories, and some healthy fat is good for you. Coat a portabella cap with a teaspoon of oil before baking, grilling, or cooking on the stove for optimum flavor. A little oil is also great on zucchini, bell peppers, and onion . . . especially when roasted or baked at a high temp!

~ RICE, PASTA, AND MORE ~

Brown Rice

As far as grains go, brown rice gets top marks. A ¼-cup serving of the uncooked grains has about 170 calories and 2 grams of fiber. That cooks up to about ¾ cup. To save time, go for instant; the dry serving size may differ, but the calorie counts per cup of cooked rice are the same. The boil-in-a-bag options are convenient and easy to use!

HG Heads-Up
Those mini microwavable containers of brown rice are great in theory, but looks can be deceiving. They often contain more than one serving! Check the labels before buying.

HG FYI:
Check the freezer aisle for steamable bags of brown rice, like the kind by Birds Eye!

HG Tips: To make the most of a single serving of brown rice, stir in tons of diced veggies, fresh or thawed from frozen. Peas, carrots, bean sprouts, broccoli cole slaw, shredded cabbage, and finely chopped cauliflower are all great for this. Another tip? Don't make rice your main course. Fill your plate with lean protein and veggies, and then enjoy a serving of fluffy rice on the side!

Whole Grain 101

Whole grains add fiber and complex carbohydrates to your diet. When the carbs are complex, they break down more slowly, keeping them in your system longer. Since your body processes them slowly, you don't crash. This also keeps your insulin levels steady—a good thing, since insulin spikes tell your body to hold on to fat. Go, grains! Great whole-grain sources in our book: brown rice, oats, and whole-wheat products. (Literally, they're all here in our book.)

BAKING PRODUCTS, PANTRY STAPLES, SPICES, AND MORE

Instant Potato Flakes

Think of these quickie carbs as a recipe starter. The flakes themselves only have about 80 calories and no fat per ⅓-cup serving. It's all about what you add! You can super-size your mashies with mashed cauliflower. And stick to guilt-free extras for creaminess, cheesiness, and flavor—things like light cheese wedges by The Laughing Cow, fat-free sour cream, and garlic powder!

High-Fiber and Whole-Wheat-Blend Pasta

When it comes to any kind of uncooked pasta, a standard 2-ounce serving has 180 to 200 calories. So look for whole-wheat-blend options with 4 to 6 grams of fiber per serving. (If you're gonna eat carb-heavy noodles, get some fiber out of the deal!) To keep calorie counts in check, stick with light sauces. See the Pasta Essentials on **page 203** for sauce suggestions!

HG FYI:
Check out the TOP ATE Items Worth Ordering Online (**page 199**) for an amazing pasta find!!

> **HG Standouts:** Ronzoni Healthy Harvest and Smart Taste, and Barilla Plus and Whole Grain.

Pasta Swaps and Super-Sizers!

House Foods Tofu Shirataki — THE pasta swap of the century. A serving has just 20 calories! Use it as a swap or a super-sizer with spaghetti, fettuccine, and angel-hair pasta. (See the next page for loads more info on this awesome item!)

Zucchini — Cut zucchini into long, thin ribbons, cook and then toss with some fettuccine.

Spaghetti Squash — Bake or boil squash halves until soft. Then scrape out the noodle-like strands inside, and toss it with spaghetti for an extra-large serving with way fewer calories! Or skip the pasta altogether!

Broccoli Cole Slaw — So easy. Steam or stir-fry, toss with crushed tomatoes or low-fat marinara, and sprinkle with reduced-fat Parm. Kicks a spaghetti craving straight to the curb!

Bean Sprouts — Amazing stir-fried or steamed until soft. An especially great addition to lo mein and other Asian-style noodle dishes!

Eggplant — If you're making lasagna, swap every other sheet of pasta for a slab of eggplant. Your lasagna will be less heavy without being any less delicious.

⭐ HG All-Star!
House Foods Tofu Shirataki Noodle Substitute

There's a lot you need to know about these noodles, a.k.a. the WORLD'S BEST PASTA SWAP. Let's start at the beginning . . .

What Are They?
These are noodles made from Japanese yam flour and tofu. They're a bit more slippery than regular noodles, but they're also SUPER-LOW in calories—each 4-ounce serving (half a bag) has 20 calories, 0.5 grams of fat, and 2 grams of fiber. That's only 40 calories for the whole 8-ounce bag!

Where to Find Them:
In the refrigerated section where the tofu and other Asian items are found. They'll be floating in liquid inside a clear bag, and they're available in shapes like fettuccine and spaghetti. If your store doesn't carry them, request 'em!

How Do I Prepare Them?

Empty your noodles into a strainer, and rinse them well to get rid of the liquid they were packed in.

Dry them as thoroughly as possible by blotting with paper towels. Remove as much moisture as possible! This greatly improves recipes and helps keep sauces from getting watered down.

Since they're VERY long, cut them up a bit. (Kitchen shears make this super-easy.)

Warm them in the microwave or in a skillet on the stove. Done!

Sauce Suggestions:
Low-fat creamy sauces are the best way to go. (The Laughing Cow Light cheese wedges are a fantastic ingredient!) They're also great stir-fried with Asian-style sauces. What doesn't work? Thin tomato-based sauces. The sauce is often too watery.

Anything Else?
It doesn't taste EXACTLY like pasta, but if you want something that walks and talks like a noodle (or wiggles and lays like a noodle) but doesn't have a boatload of carbs and calories, Tofu Shirataki will be your new BFF.

HG SHOCKER!

> 8 ounces of cooked pasta has **TEN TIMES** as many calories as 8 ounces of Tofu Shirataki noodles.

BAKING PRODUCTS, PANTRY STAPLES, SPICES, AND MORE

Wonton Wrappers

These are found in the refrigerated section with the tofu and Asian foods. Wonton wrappers are super-thin squares of dough, floured and ready to use. Each one has about 20 calories and no fat. They're good for both savory and sweet items, since they're basically little edible blank slates.

Recipe Idea: Wrap them around your filling of choice and seal the edges together; then cook in a skillet or bake in the oven for potsticker-like appetizers.

Super-Easy Recipe Idea: Press them into the cups of a muffin pan sprayed with nonstick spray, and bake into crunchy 20-calorie shells to be filled with anything you like!

HG Trick: Have a small dish of water out before you start working with wonton or egg roll wrappers. To seal, dip your finger in water and run it across one of the edges. Firmly press the edges together, and continue on without interruption!

Egg Roll Wrappers

These are essentially larger versions of wonton wrappers, with about 60 calories each. Great for making your very own egg rolls—just wrap up your goodies, and bake instead of frying for guilt-free appetizers! Get creative with unconventional fillings like fruit mixed with a little pudding and shredded chicken mixed with cheese.

Wrap N Roll:
HG's Mini Guide to Egg Roll Wrapping!

Traditional Egg Roll Style — Spoon filling onto the wrapper in a row a little below center. Moisten all 4 edges of the wrapper, and fold the sides in about ¾ inch toward the filling. Roll the bottom of each wrapper around the filling, keep rolling until you reach the top, and seal the outside edge with water.

Super-Easy Taquito Style — Spoon filling onto wrapper and spread evenly over the entire surface. Roll up tightly into a cigar-shaped tube and, if needed, secure with toothpicks.

Pocket Style — Spoon filling onto the bottom half of each wrapper. Moisten all 4 edges of the wrapper, and fold the top half over the filling, so the top edge meets the bottom. Press edges firmly to seal.

Bake until crispy, and prepare to chew!

~ SWEETENERS, ETC. ~

* NEED-TO-KNOW LINGO *
NO-CALORIE SWEETENER PACKETS EDITION

Saccharin

Alias: Sweet'N Low
Found In: Pink packets.

Possibly conjuring images of 1960s diner coffee, these packets aren't as popular as they once were, being edged out by the other sweeteners listed below. They still have some die-hard fans though.

Aspartame

Aliases: NutraSweet, Equal
Found In: Blue packets.

If you consume a lot of sugar-free products, you're probably very used to the taste of aspartame. These blue packets have been sitting alongside the pink ones for decades.

Sucralose

Alias: Splenda
Found In: Yellow packets.
Derived from sugar, and some feel it tastes most like the real thing.

Stevia

Aliases: Truvia, Pure Via, Reb A
Found In: Green packets (or sometimes white packets with green writing).

This is the hot sweetener of the moment. It's natural and comes from the stevia plant. Fair warning: Some stevia products can be a tad bitter.

No-Calorie Sweetener Packets

Like so many "zero-calorie" items, these do contain some calories. On average, each packet has 4 calories. Still less than ⅓rd of the calories in a packet of sugar. Use these to sweeten more than just your coffee and tea. Add them to plain fat-free yogurt (Greek or regular), fat-free cottage cheese, blended beverages, cold cereal, hot cereal, and more. The great thing about no-calorie sweetener packets is that there are options for everyone.

> **HG Standouts:** Splenda has been the go-to no-calorie sweetener for ages, and **Truvia** is our stevia pick.

HG All-Natural Picks: In addition to Truvia, try Pure Via, Stevia Extract In The Raw, and Sun Crystals (a stevia/sugar combo with five calories per packet).

Splenda No Calorie Sweetener, Granulated

We'll bottom-line it for you: A full cup of granulated Splenda has 96 calories. A cup of granulated sugar has 775 calories. If you plan to bake something that calls for a lot of sugar, you can save a tremendous amount of calories by using this instead. And since this product is specifically meant for baking, it has a nice light texture and measures cup-for-cup like sugar. Swap all of the sugar in a recipe for an equal amount of Splenda, or find a ratio that works for you. Either way, you'll be cutting calories.

HG Alternative: Prefer to keep things all natural? Stevia Extract In The Raw's Cup for Cup granulated sweetener comes loose in the bag, just like Splenda's granulated stuff. Used in recipes in place of Splenda or sugar, it's not bad. It's a bit sweeter than Splenda's version, so keep that in mind. Some other stevia brands make similar products too.

Powdered Sugar

Hugely underrated product here! Powdered sugar is the sweet, fluffy, white kind that pretty much melts when it touches your tongue. Since it's lighter in weight than regular sugar, it actually has ⅓rd fewer calories when measured. AMAZING! A teaspoon of powdered sugar has just 10 calories. Use it as a topping for breakfast items like waffles, pancakes, and French toast. Top off warm desserts with it. Sprinkle it over parfaits and fruit. Totally indulgent and completely delicious!

Granulated White Sugar

It's all about moderation, people. If you're only using a little bit, it's okay to use real sugar. It tastes great! A level teaspoon has about 15 calories. Try mixing real sugar with granulated Splenda if you're whipping up something that requires a lot of sweetener but you want to keep excess calories at bay.

Brown Sugar

When you need brown sugar taste, there's really no substitute for the real thing. Use small amounts of brown sugar for a rich, buttery taste in baked goods and even savory sauces. A teaspoon of lightly packed brown sugar has about 15 calories.

What About Splenda Brown Sugar Blend and Splenda for Baking? Splenda Brown Sugar Blend is merely a mix of granulated Splenda No Calorie Sweetener and regular brown sugar. Splenda for Baking is a combo of Splenda and white sugar. So if you already buy boxes of regular granulated Splenda, buying regular (cheaper) brown and white sugar is a way to save a little money. Plus, you'll have more control over the sugar-to-Splenda ratio, which is nice.

Sugar-Free Calorie-Free Flavored Syrups

These aren't thick syrups. They're liquidy, which makes them perfect for hot drinks, cold cocktails, and more. They're ideal any time you want to add fun sweet flavor without a lot of calories. These are available online in a slew of crazy flavors, but look for common ones like vanilla in the coffee aisle . . . Just make sure they're the zero-calorie, sugar-free kinds, because there are sugary versions too! (Pssst . . . They can also be found at specialty stores like Cost Plus World Market and BevMo!)

HG Snack Ideas: Add a little vanilla syrup to fat-free "egg wash" when making French toast, and you'll have a vanilla-infused breakfast. Stir some into yogurt, cottage cheese, and even oatmeal. You can even drizzle a small amount over fruit or ice cream. Get creative!

> **HG Standout:** Torani Sugar Free. See page 199 for more info!

BAKING PRODUCTS, PANTRY STAPLES, SPICES, AND MORE

Sugar-Free and Fat-Free Flavored Powdered Creamer

Not only are these good in coffee (which is kind of a given!), they're an amazing way to give a boost of sweet creaminess to almost anything in need. Shakes, oatmeal bowls, hot cocoa, smoothies . . . even batters for baked goods. The sugar-free kind is slightly lower in calories than the fat-free stuff, but they're both amazing and impressive and can be used interchangeably. A tablespoon of the sugar-free kind has around 30 calories and 2.5 grams of fat; the fat-free kind has about 40 per tablespoon. The vanilla flavor's our MVP!

HG Standouts: Coffee-mate Sugar Free and Fat Free French Vanilla powdered creamers. Hands-down favorites!

HG Tip: Some of the best flavors hit shelves in winter around the holidays, so stock up; powdered creamer has a long shelf life!

HG Powdered Creamer Tip!

If you're adding it to something cold (that won't be heated), dissolve the creamer in a small amount of hot water first. No one likes creamer lumps . . .

Fat-Free Plain Powdered Creamer

INSANELY creamy. Just like the flavored kind, but useful in recipes that don't require sweetness. A tablespoon or two can do wonders for a creamy soup or sauce. It's actually a great way to infuse velvety texture into mashed potatoes! (See Instant Potato Flakes on page 188 to see how we bulk ours up with cauliflower!)

> **HG Standout:** Coffee-mate Fat Free The Original powdered creamer.

Why Powdered Flavored Creamer and Not Liquid?
When it comes to sugar-free and fat-free flavored creamer, both the liquid and powdered versions are creamy and sweet with impressive stats. But the powdered version is a MUCH better kitchen staple. For one thing, portion control. While recipes make it easy and call for specific amounts of creamer, it's WAY too easy to over-pour liquid creamer into your coffee, causing calories to rack up quickly. (No one uses just ONE tablespoon!) With the powder, a little goes a long way, and it's easier to keep the amount you're adding in check. Also, the powdered creamer has a much longer shelf life; so if you're not someone who drinks coffee daily but you want to make an HG recipe or two with the stuff, you're much better off buying the powdered kind. Same goes for plain, unflavored creamer—just make sure to get the fat-free version!

BAKING PRODUCTS, PANTRY STAPLES, SPICES, AND MORE

HG's TOP ATE
Spices and Extracts

Assorted seasonings, dried herbs, and extracts are all great ways to add flavor for hardly any calories. Here are eight must-haves that you'll want to use in everything. You can't beat the basics . . .

1. Vanilla extract
2. Coconut extract
3. Cinnamon
4. Garlic powder
5. Onion powder
6. Italian seasoning
7. Dried minced onion
8. Pumpkin pie spice

Dry Taco, Fajita, and Chili Seasoning Mix

You know that aisle in the grocery store full of little paper packets of powder? Get to know it better! If you're in a hurry and want your food of choice to taste like taco, adding a bit of seasoning will do the trick in a snap. And don't feel bound by the food named on the package. You can add these flavors ANYWHERE you want them. Veggies, scrambles, sauces, stir-frys . . . Stock up on your favorite blends, keep 'em on hand, and try adding a bit here and there in your quickie cooking. SO EASY! A teaspoon has about 10 calories.

Salt-Slashing 411: If you're a sodium-watcher, look for low-sodium mixes. There are also salt-free blends on shelves, like the kind by Mrs. Dash.

Dry Onion Soup/Dip Mix

It's not just for making soups and dips. Use it to season chicken, sauces, veggies, and other items in a flash. And don't think you need to use the whole packet at once or not at all—just keep an opened packet in a sealable baggie for next time. A tablespoon of the mix itself has about 20 calories and no fat.

Dry Ranch Dressing/Dip Mix

Truth time: Bottled fat-free ranch dressing doesn't always taste great. For fantastic ranch taste, turn to the dry mix. It has about 30 fat-free calories per tablespoon, and its intense delicious flavor goes far. Use a little as a seasoning—it's great rubbed onto raw lean chicken breast cutlets before you cook them. Mix it with fat-free sour cream or fat-free yogurt for a dressing/dip hybrid. Or combine it with ground meat—lean turkey or extra-lean beef—for ranch-ified burger patties!

Jarred Chopped Garlic

When you need more flavor than garlic powder can provide, but you can't be bothered to chop garlic yourself, jarred garlic is a great item to have. Punch up the flavor of savory dishes, and all you have to do is scoop. Generally, you can find both chopped and crushed versions; be careful, because the crushed stuff is super-potent. And make sure you don't grab garlic that's packed in oil. (Really, what's the point?)

HG'S TOP ATE
ITEMS WORTH ORDERING ONLINE!

1. Powdered Peanut Butter (PB2 and FitNutz)

Mixed with water, powdered PB gets creamy. A 2-tablespoon serving has just 45 to 50 calories and 1.5 grams of fat, which is a fraction of the calories of regular peanut butter. It's a little sweet, and it works wonders as an ingredient in shakes, oatmeal, dessert toppings, and more.

bellplantation.com and fitnutzbutter.com

2. Vitalicious VitaTops (Full Flavor Lineup!)

Many markets carry a few flavors of these fiber-packed muffin tops (in the freezer aisle). For options like Apple Crumb and the HG-developed Fudgy Peanut Butter Chip and Triple Chocolate Chunk VitaTops, these are definitely worth ordering online. They'll obliterate cravings for brownies, cakes, cookies, and more. And for just 90 to 100 calories and 1 to 2.5 grams of fat!

vitalicious.com

3. FiberGourmet Light Pasta

These wonder noodles have only 130 calories and a whopping 18 grams of fiber per serving . . . that's 40 percent fewer calories than standard pasta! And they come in a variety of shapes and sizes, from penne to lasagna.

FiberGourmet.com

4. Healthy Snackin's Simply Snackin Dried Gourmet Meat Snacks

This stuff is unbelievably delicious and super-schmancy. Each individually wrapped, protein-packed snack has just 50 calories and 1 to 2 grams of fat. You'll find all-natural chicken breast and beef sirloin with dried fruit, cheese, and more. The ultimate on-the-go snack!

healthysnackin.com

5. Vivi's Original Sauce Classic Carnival Mustard

This completely unique stuff is part mustard, part relish, part salsa, part hot sauce. It's fantastic as a spread or a dip. Each tablespoon has just 15 calories and no fat whatsoever! IT ROCKS!

vivisoriginalsauce.com

6. Torani Sugar Free Syrups

With more than thirty flavors to choose from, these zero-calorie, sugarless syrups are crucial to making guilt-free cocktails, blended beverages, and hot drinks. Also stir some into your yogurt, cottage cheese, or oatmeal for fun flavor. Top flavor picks: Coconut, Black Cherry, Mango, and Raspberry!

torani.com

7. Lucero Flavored Balsamic Vinegars

Sweet balsamic vinegar infused with fruity flavors like blueberry, peach, and wild cherry? Amazing! Try some drizzled over berries or grilled veggies. Just 25 fat-free calories per tablespoon.

luceroliveoil.com

8. FRS Low Calorie Orange Concentrate

Mixed with water and served over crushed ice, you've got a delicious drink that's packed with vitamins and antioxidants. Energizing and just 15 calories a serving. Fair warning: Don't sign up for AutoShip unless you really want it.

frs.com

BONUS SECTION: HG ESSENTIALS!

YOUR AT-A-GLANCE GUIDE TO CREATING OODLES OF DELICIOUS GUILT-FREE MEALS AND SIPS!

BURGER ESSENTIALS

Burgers

Meatless hamburger-style or veggie-burger patties with
100 calories or less
Breaded-chicken-style soy patties (Boca, Morningstar Farms)
Large portabella mushrooms (the original vegetarian burger swap!)
Lean turkey burger patties (Jennie-O, Butterball)
Extra-lean ground beef (about 96% lean)
Lean ground turkey (about 93% lean)

Buns

Light and high-fiber buns
100-calorie flat sandwich buns
Light English muffins
Lettuce leaves (for low-carb burgers!)
Light bread (45 calories per slice)
Large high-fiber flour tortillas with about 110 calories each

Condiments

Ketchup
Assorted mustards
Hellmann's/Best Foods Dijonnaise
Light, reduced-fat, or fat-free mayo
BBQ sauce with about 45 calories per serving
Hot sauce
Thick teriyaki marinade with 30 or fewer calories
per tablespoon
Salsa

Toppings

Fat-free and reduced-fat cheese slices
The Laughing Cow Light cheese wedges
Lettuce leaves
Onion
Tomatoes (big tomato = big slices)
Avocado (use sparingly!)
Pickle chips
Jarred roasted red peppers
Jarred jalapeño slices
Canned pineapple rings packed in juice (AMAZING grilled!)
Center-cut bacon or turkey bacon
Spices (for seasoning raw ground meat!)

PASTA ESSENTIALS

Sauces
Canned crushed tomatoes
Frank's RedHot Original Cayenne Pepper Sauce
(just a little adds an extra kick!)
Amy's Organic Chunky Tomato Bisque
The Laughing Cow Light Creamy Swiss cheese wedges with
fat-free sour cream (great Alfredo sauce swap!)
Frozen broccoli in cheese sauce
(toss with noodles for a guilt-free mac & cheese swap!)
Reduced-fat Parmesan-style grated topping

Noodles & Noodle Swaps
House Foods Tofu Shirataki Noodle Substitute
(best in creamy sauces)
Whole-wheat pasta
Spaghetti squash
Zucchini (thinly slice into ribbons and add to fettuccine!)
Broccoli cole slaw (just stir-fry until limp, and toss with red sauce)

COFFEE DRINK ESSENTIALS

Coffee
Ground or whole coffee beans
(brew your coffee extra-strong if you're icing it!)
Instant coffee granules
(for cold drinks, dissolve in a small amount of hot liquid first!)

Milk & Creamers
Unsweetened Vanilla Almond Breeze
(for making the most guilt-free lattes EVER)
Light vanilla soymilk
Sugar-free/fat-free flavored powdered creamers

Sweeteners & Syrups
No-calorie sweetener packets, like Splenda or Truvia
(or your reduced-calorie sweetener of choice)
Sugar-free calorie-free flavored syrups (like Torani Sugar Free!)

Other Items
Unsweetened cocoa powder
Hot cocoa packets with around 25 calories each
Fat Free Reddi-wip
Light/fat-free caramel dip (frequently found in the produce section)
Light/sugar-free chocolate syrup
Extracts (vanilla, almond, coconut, peppermint, etc.)
Mini semi-sweet chocolate chips
(melted into hot coffee, they really boost a DIY mocha!)
Bendy straws (a must!)

PIZZA ESSENTIALS

Sauce Options

Jarred pizza sauce

Canned crushed tomatoes (seasoned if available)

Canned tomato sauce

Canned low-fat chunky tomato soup
(like Amy's Organic Chunky Tomato Bisque)

The Laughing Cow Light cheese wedges (white pizza!)

BBQ sauce (BBQ chicken pizza!)

Salsa or taco sauce (Mexican pizza!)

Pizza Bottom Options

Large high-fiber flour tortillas with about 110 calories each

Light English muffins (split 'em and make mini pizzas)

Light/high-fiber pitas

100-calorie flat sandwich buns
(like English muffin pizzas, but larger!)

Pillsbury Classic Pizza Crust dough

Portabella mushrooms

Bell peppers (the bigger the better)

Eggplant (top large slabs of eggplant like a pizza;
you'll have to eat 'em with a fork though)

Chicken breast (pound it thin, cook, then top it like a pizza!)

Fat-free egg substitute (cook flat in a skillet without stirring,
and then top it like a pizza!)

Cheese Options

Light string cheese (pull into strings and chop; or put in a
blender and blitz!)

Shredded fat-free/part-skim mozzarella cheese

Reduced-fat Parmesan-style grated topping

Other fat-free/reduced-fat cheeses (American for a cheeseburger
pizza, pepper jack for a southwestern pizza!)

Toppings

Thinly sliced fresh veggies

Turkey pepperoni

Ground-beef-style soy crumbles (by Morningstar Farms or Boca)

Canadian bacon

Turkey bacon or center-cut bacon
(cooked and chopped or crumbled)

Soy chorizo (SO much flavor, and SO much less fat than
the real thing)

Canned sliced olives

Jarred sliced jalapeños (if you like it hot!)

Hot sauce

Spices (garlic powder, onion powder, crushed red pepper,
Italian seasoning)

Chopped pineapple (Hawaiian pizza!)

EGG-MUG/EGG-SCRAMBLE ESSENTIALS

Basics

Nonstick spray (your skillet or microwave-safe mug will be easier to clean!)

Light whipped butter or light buttery spread

Fat-free liquid egg substitute (liquid egg whites work fine too)

Cheeses

The Laughing Cow Light cheese wedges

Shredded fat-free or reduced-fat cheese

Reduced-fat Parmesan-style grated topping

Meaty Mix-ins

Extra-lean deli meat (chopped!)

Ground-beef-style soy crumbles (by Morningstar Farms or Boca)

Meatless hamburger-style or veggie-burger patties with 100 calories or less (chopped!)

Turkey pepperoni

Center-cut bacon or turkey bacon

Precooked real crumbled bacon

Canadian bacon

Meatless or lean turkey sausage

Canned low-fat turkey or veggie chili

Soy chorizo

Veggie Picks

Spinach (fresh or frozen)

Bell peppers and onions (for fajita-like egg creations)

Mushrooms

Chopped tomatoes (patted dry)

Canned diced green chiles

Jarred jalapeño peppers

Condiments

Ketchup

Salsa

Frank's RedHot Original Cayenne Pepper Sauce

Fat-free sour cream

Enchilada sauce

Taco sauce

Dry Spices

Italian seasoning

Garlic powder

Onion powder

Dried minced onion

Taco seasoning mix

THE **COMPLETE** HUNGRY GIRL SUPERMARKET LIST!

DAIRY

Cheese

- **Fat-free and reduced-fat shredded cheese**
  Kraft, Sargento, Weight Watchers
- **Fat-free and reduced-fat slices**
  Kraft, Sargento, Weight Watchers
- **Fat-free and reduced-fat block-style cheese**
  Lifetime, Cabot
- **Reduced-fat cheese snacks with 100 calories or less**
  Mini Babybel (regular and Light), Kraft 100 Calorie Packs
  Cheese Bites, Weight Watchers, Cabot Serious Snacking
- **Light string cheese**
  Frigo, Sargento, Weight Watchers
- **Fat-free and reduced-fat crumbled feta cheese**
  Athenos, Président
- **The Laughing Cow Light cheese wedges**
- **Fat-free cream cheese in a tub**
  Philadelphia
- **Fat-free, low-fat, and light (not part-skim) ricotta cheese**
  Frigo, Precious
- **Fat-free and low-fat cottage cheese**
  Knudsen/Breakstone's On the Go!/Snack Size, Fiber One
- **Fat-free and low-fat cottage cheese with fruit**
  Knudsen/Breakstone's Doubles
- **Almond cheese and soy cheese (low in fat)**
  Lisanatti Foods The Original Almond Cheese Alternative, Galaxy Veggie
- **Reduced-fat Parmesan-style grated topping (pasta aisle)**
  Kraft

Yogurt

- **Fat-free fruity and desserty yogurt**
  Yoplait Light, Yoplait Fiber One, Dannon Light & Fit, Weight Watchers
- **Fat-free plain yogurt**
- **Fat-free and reduced-fat plain Greek yogurt**
  Fage Total 0%, Fage Total 2%, Chobani 0%, Chobani 2%
- **Fat-free and reduced-fat Greek yogurt with fruit**
  Fage Total 0% with Fruit, Fage Total 2% with Fruit, Chobani 0% with
  Fruit, Chobani 2% with Fruit, Athenos 0% with Fruit

Pudding, Desserts, and Dessert Toppings

- **Sugar-free and no-sugar-added pudding snack cups**
  Jell-O Sugar Free, Handi-Snacks Sugar Free, Snack Pack Sugar Free or No Sugar Added
- **Mousse Temptations by Jell-O**
- **No-sugar-added rice pudding**
  Kozy Shack
- **No-sugar-added tapioca pudding**
  Kozy Shack
- **Sugar-free gelatin snack cups**
  Jell-O Sugar Free
- **Fat Free Reddi-wip**
- **Cool Whip Free (freezer aisle)**

Egg Products

- **Fat-free liquid egg substitute**
  Egg Beaters Original, Better'n Eggs, Nulaid ReddiEgg
- **Liquid egg whites**
  AllWhites, Egg Beaters Whites
- **Eggs (for making hard-boiled whites)**

Milk, Milk Swaps, and Creamers

- **Blue Diamond Unsweetened Vanilla Almond Breeze (refrigerated or shelf-stable)**
- **Light vanilla soymilk**
  8th Continent Light, Silk Light
- **Unsweetened coconut milk beverage**
  So Delicious (refrigerated or shelf-stable)
- **Fat-free non-dairy liquid creamer**
  Coffee-mate The Original Fat Free

Sour Cream and Butter

- **Fat-free sour cream**
- **Light buttery spread and light whipped butter in a tub**
  Brummel & Brown, Land O' Lakes Whipped Light, Smart Balance Light
- **I Can't Believe It's Not Butter! Spray**

CEREAL

Cold Cereal

- **Fiber One Original bran cereal**
- **Puffed rice**
- **Puffed wheat**
  Kashi 7 Whole Grain Puffs
- **Puffed corn**
  Kix
- **Other cereals with about 150 calories and at least 4 grams of fiber per 1-cup serving**
  Kashi Squares Honey Sunshine, Barbara's Bakery Puffins, Kashi Heart to Heart Warm Cinnamon Oat Cereal, Cinnamon Burst Cheerios, Chocolate Cheerios, Fiber One (all varieties)
- **Kid classics (sweet stuff)**
  Cap'n Crunch, Reese's Puffs
- **Single-serving cereal boxes**

Hot Cereal

- **Old-fashioned oats**
  Quaker
- **Instant oatmeal packets**
  Quaker, Kashi, Nature's Path Organic

MEAT AND SEAFOOD

Poultry

Jimmy Dean, Jennie-O, Butterball, Foster Farms, Perdue

- **Boneless skinless lean chicken breast and turkey breast (raw uncooked breasts, tenders, and cutlets; precooked cutlets, strips, and chopped)**
- **Lean ground turkey**
- **Lean turkey burger patties (refrigerated and frozen)**
- **Lean turkey sausage**
- **Turkey pepperoni**
  Hormel

Beef

Laura's Lean Beef

- Extra-lean ground beef
- Extra-lean steak (top round, top sirloin)
- Lean steak (strip, tenderloin, t-bone, shoulder)

Pork

- Extra-lean pork (tenderloin)
- Lean pork (top loin chops, top loin roast, center loin chops, center rib chops, and sirloin roast)

Bacon

Oscar Mayer, Hormel, Jennie-O, Applegate

- Center-cut bacon
- Turkey bacon
- Precooked real crumbled bacon
- Imitation bacon bits
- Canadian bacon

Packaged and Deli Meats

- Extra-lean turkey breast, chicken breast, ham, and roast beef slices
  Boar's Head, Oscar Mayer, Applegate, Butterball, Healthy Ones, Sara Lee

Hot Dogs

- 97% to 100% fat-free hot dogs
  Hoffy Extra Lean Beef Franks, Hebrew National 97% Fat Free Beef Franks, Ball Park Fat Free, Ball Park Bun Size Smoked White Turkey

Seafood

- Tilapia, tuna, and other lean fish fillets
- Salmon
- Smoked salmon (a.k.a. lox)
- Shrimp
- Scallops
- Crab
  Chicken of the Sea Lump Crab, Trade Winds, MeTompkin
- Imitation crabmeat

Shelf-Stable Seafood and Other Proteins

- Canned and pouched albacore tuna (packed in water)
- Canned and pouched boneless and skinless pink salmon (packed in water)
- Pouched seasoned tuna and salmon
  StarKist Salmon, Albacore & Tuna Creations
- Pouched ready-to-serve seasoned albacore and salmon (packed in water)
  Bumble Bee Prime Fillet Albacore Steak Entrées
- Canned 98% fat-free chunk white chicken breast (packed in water)

MEAT SUBSTITUTES

Burger and Beef Swaps

- Frozen meatless hamburger-style patties
  Boca Original Vegan, Amy's Bistro, Morningstar Farms Grillers Vegan Veggie
- Frozen meatless veggie-burger patties
  Gardenburger, Boca, Amy's, Morningstar Farms, Dr. Praeger's
- Frozen ground-beef-style soy crumbles
  Boca Meatless Ground Crumbles, Morningstar Farms Meal Starters Grillers Recipe Crumbles
- Meatless meatballs (frozen and refrigerated)
  Veggie Patch, Nate's

Sausage Swaps

- Frozen meatless sausage-style breakfast patties and links
  Morningstar Farms
- Refrigerated soy chorizo, a.k.a. soyrizo
  El Burrito, Melissa's, Frieda's

Chicken Swaps

- Faux grilled chicken patties, cutlets, and strips (frozen and refrigerated)
  Morningstar Farms, Lightlife
- Frozen breaded-chicken-style soy patties
  Boca, Morningstar Farms

Meatless Novelties

- **Frozen meatless corn dogs**
  Morningstar Farms
- **Meatless Buffalo wings (frozen and refrigerated)**
  Morningstar Farms, Lightlife
- **Frozen meatless chicken nuggets**
  Morningstar Farms
- **Frozen Morningstar Farms Hickory BBQ Riblets**

PRODUCE

Fresh Vegetables

- Artichokes
- Asparagus
- Bell peppers
- Broccoli
- Brussels sprouts
- Butternut squash
- Cabbage
- Carrots
- Cauliflower
- Celery
- Cucumbers
- Eggplant
- Jicama
- Kabocha squash
- Kale
- Lettuce
- Mushrooms
- Onions
- Scallions
- Snow peas and sugar snap peas
- Spaghetti squash

Fresh Vegetables cont.

- Spinach
- Tomatoes
- Turnips
- Zucchini and crookneck squash

Bagged Produce

- Salad mixes
- Broccoli cole slaw
- Classic cole slaw mix
- Bean sprouts
- Chopped & prepared veggies/veggie snacks
  Mann's Snacks on the Go!

Herbs

- Dill
- Basil
- Mint
- Parsley
- Cilantro

Frozen Vegetables

- Stir-fry veggies
- Potatoes O'Brien
  Ore-Ida
- Petite mixed vegetables
- Cauliflower and broccoli florets
- Mashed winter squash
- Chopped spinach
- Edamame
- Seasoned veggies and veggies in low-fat sauce
  Green Giant Just for One, Green Giant Health Blends
- Steam-in-the-bag veggies
  Birds Eye, Green Giant, Veg-All

Fresh Fruit

- Apples
- Avocados
- Bananas
- Berries
- Cherries
- Clementines
- Cranberries
- Grapefruits
- Grapes
- Mangos
- Melons
- Nectarines
- Oranges
- Peaches
- Pears
- Plums

Frozen Fruit

- No-sugar-added strawberries
- No-sugar-added dark sweet cherries
- No-sugar-added mango chunks
- No-sugar-added peach slices
- No-sugar-added mixed berries

And pretty much any fruit or veggie we may have left off of this list!

CANNED FOODS

Fruit

- Pineapple packed in juice (chunks, tidbits, crushed, slices/rings)
- Mandarin oranges packed in juice
- Peach slices packed in juice
- Fruit packed in water
  Del Monte No Sugar Added
- No-sugar-added applesauce
- Pure pumpkin
  Libby's 100%
- Fruit purees (find in the baby foods aisle)

Tomatoes
Muir Glen Organic, Hunt's

- Crushed tomatoes
- Tomato sauce
- Tomato paste
- Diced tomatoes
- Stewed tomatoes
- Sun-dried tomatoes (packed in oil or pouches)

Vegetables

- Sweet peas
- Sweet corn kernels
  Green Giant Mexicorn
- Jarred roasted red peppers
- Sliced jalapeño peppers (or banana peppers)
- Sliced beets
- Artichoke hearts and bottoms
- Sliced black olives
- Pickles (refrigerated or shelf-stable)
- Relish
- Sauerkraut
- Hearts of palm

Latin Foods

- Chipotle peppers in adobo sauce
- Mild green chiles

Asian Foods

- Bamboo shoots
- Water chestnuts
- Straw mushrooms

Soup

- **Low-calorie soups**
  Amy's Organic, Amy's Organic Light in Sodium, Progresso 99%
  Fat Free, Progresso Light, Progresso High Fiber, Campbell's Soup
  at Hand (check stats for low-fat ones), Campbell's V8 Soups

- **Low-fat creamy tomato soup**
  Amy's Organic Chunky Tomato Bisque (and Light in Sodium version, too!)

- **Instant soups**
  Mishima (Miso & Edamame!)

- **Low-fat turkey and veggie chili**
  Amy's, Hormel, Health Valley, Kettle Cuisine (in freezer aisle)

- **Fat-free chicken, beef, and vegetable broth (look for low-sodium)**

- **98% fat-free cream of celery, chicken, and mushroom
  condensed soups**
  Campbell's

- **Freezer-aisle soups**
  Tabatchnick, Kettle Cuisine

Beans

- **Black beans**
- **Red kidney beans**
- **Cannellini (a.k.a. white kidney) beans**
- **Garbanzo beans (a.k.a. chickpeas)**
- **Fat-free or low-fat refried beans**

PACKAGED SNACKS

Crackers, Chips, and Other Crunchy Snacks

- **High-fiber crackers (especially flatbread-style)**
  Wheat Thins Fiber Selects, Ryvita, Wasa, Dr. Kracker Flatbreads

- **Reduced-fat baked and popped potato chips**
  Popchips, Kettle Brand Baked, Baked! Lay's, Pringles Light,
  Cape Cod 40% Reduced Fat/Less Fat, Michael Season's Baked
  single-serving snacks

- **Low-fat baked tortilla chips**
  Guiltless Gourmet, Baked! Tostitos Scoops!

- **Hard pretzels**
  Snack Factory Pretzel Crisps

Rice snacks and soy crisps
Quaker Quakes, Quaker Mini Delights, Quaker Tortillaz, Genisoy
Soy Crisps, Glenny's Soy Crisps

Rice cakes
Quaker

94% fat-free microwave popcorn bags
Jolly Time Healthy Pop, Orville Redenbacher's SmartPop!, Pop Secret
100 Calorie Pop

Freeze-dried fruit
Gerber Graduates Mini Fruits, Just Tomatoes, Etc.!, Funky Monkey,
Crispy Green, Sensible Foods

100-calorie snack packs & treats
Nabisco 100 Cal, Hostess 100 Calorie Packs, Entenmann's Little
Bites, Kellogg's 100 Calorie Right Bites, Chex 100 Calorie, Frito-Lay
Mini Bites, Weight Watchers Snack Cakes, Rice Krispies Treats The
Original Bars, Pringles Stix

Snack Bars

Cereal bars & chewy granola bars
Quaker, Fiber One, Special K, Kashi, Soyjoy Bars

Crunchy granola bars
Nature Valley, Kashi TLC Crunchy Granola

Decadent snack bars
Fiber One, Special K, Chex Mix

"Mini-meal" bars
Kashi GoLean, Kind Bars, Luna Bars, Larabars, Corazonas
Oatmeal Squares

Nuts

Pistachios in the shell
Everybody's Nuts!, Wonderful Pistachios

Almonds: whole and sliced
All Natural Almond Accents, 100-calorie packs of Blue Diamond
Almonds, 100-calorie packs of Emerald almonds

Jerky

Beef, chicken, and meatless jerky
Jack Link's, Tillamook Country Smoker, Oh Boy! Oberto,
Tasty Eats (non-chicken flavors), Primal Spirit Foods

BREAD

Slices

- **Light bread slices**
  Weight Watchers, Nature's Own Light, Nature's Own Double Fiber, Arnold Bakery Light, Sara Lee Delightful, Pepperidge Farm (Light Style, Very Thin, and Whole Grain), Fiber One

Buns

- **Light and high-fiber hamburger buns**
  Sara Lee Delightful, Nature's Own Double Fiber, Pepperidge Farm Classic

- **100-calorie flat sandwich buns**
  Arnold Select/Oroweat Sandwich Thins, Pepperidge Farm Deli Flats, Nature's Own Sandwich Rounds, EarthGrains Thin Buns, Weight Watchers Rye Flat Rolls

- **Light and high-fiber hot dog buns**
  Sara Lee Delightful, Nature's Own Double Fiber, Pepperidge Farm Classic

English Muffins

- **Light English muffins**
  Thomas', Western Bagel Alternative, Weight Watchers, Fiber One

Pita

- **Light and high-fiber pitas**
  Western Bagel Alternative, Weight Watchers

Tortillas and Flatbreads

- **Large high-fiber flour tortillas with about 110 calories each**
  La Tortilla Factory Smart & Delicious Low Carb High Fiber (Large), La Tortilla Factory 100 Calorie, Mission Carb Balance, Tumaro's 8-Inch Healthy, Tumaro's 8-Inch Low in Carbs

- **Light high-fiber flatbreads**
  Flatout Light

- **Flatout Foldit Flatbreads**

- **6-inch corn tortillas**

Taco Shells

- **Corn taco shells**

Bagels
- **Light bagels**
  Western Bagel Alternative, Weight Watchers, Thomas' Bagel Thins, Kim's Light

Specialty Items
- **Pillsbury Crescent Recipe Creations Seamless Dough Sheet (refrigerated)**
- **Pillsbury Classic Pizza Crust dough (refrigerated)**
- **Pillsbury Reduced Fat Crescent Rolls dough**
- **Lavash bread (bakery section)**
- **Ready-made dessert crepes (produce aisle)**
  Frieda's, Melissa's

FROZEN MEALS AND MEAL STARTERS

Breakfast Finds
- **Low-fat waffles**
  Kashi GoLean, Eggo Low Fat, Van's Lite
- **Breakfast sandwiches, bowls, and wraps**
  Kraft Bagel-fuls, Weight Watchers Smart Ones Morning Express,
  Jimmy Dean D-Lights Breakfast Sandwiches and Bowls, Cedarlane
  Egg White Omelettes and Breakfast Burritos, Amy's Hot Cereal Bowls
- **Vitalicious VitaTops**

Sandwiches, Etc.
- **Flatbreads, panini, and pocket sandwiches**
  Amy's Pocket Sandwiches, Lean Pockets, Lean Cuisine (Flatbread
  Melts and Panini), Weight Watchers Smart Ones Flatbreads
- **Burritos and wraps**
  Amy's, Cedarlane

Pizza
- **Multi-serving pizzas**
  Kashi, Amy's
- **Single-serving pizzas**
  Lean Cuisine, Weight Watchers Smart Ones, Amy's

Entrées

- **Classic entrées**
  Kashi, Healthy Choice, Lean Cuisine, Cedarlane, Amy's, Morningstar Farms
- **Steam-ready meals**
  Lean Cuisine Market Creations, Healthy Choice Café Steamers
- **Amy's Mexican Tamale Pie**
- **Kashi Mayan Harvest Bake**
- **Amy's Cheese Pizza Toaster Pops**
- **Contessa Stir-Fry Meals**
- **Amy's Shepherd's Pie**

ICE CREAM & FROZEN DESSERTS

Ice Cream

- **Light and fat-free ice cream cartons**
  Dreyer's/Edy's Slow Churned Light, Breyers Smooth & Dreamy Fat Free
- **Portion-controlled cups of light ice cream**
  Skinny Cow, Weight Watchers, Dreyer's/Edy's

Ice Cream Novelties

- **Light and low-fat ice cream bars**
  Skinny Cow (especially Truffle Bars!), Breyers Smooth & Dreamy
- **Low-fat ice cream sandwiches**
  Skinny Cow, Weight Watchers, Klondike Slim-a-Bear, Breyers Smooth & Dreamy
- **Light and low-fat ice cream cones**
  Weight Watchers, Skinny Cow, Nestlé Lil' Drums
- **Low-fat fudge bars**
  Weight Watchers Giant, Skinny Cow, Healthy Choice Premium, No Sugar Added Fudgsicles

Fruity Options

- **Fruit bars**
  Blue Bunny FrozFruit, Fruitfull Juice Bars, Dreyer's/Edy's Fruit Bars
- **Sorbet and light ice cream bars**
  Weight Watchers Giant Sorbet & Ice Cream Bars, Healthy Choice Premium Sorbet & Cream Bars, No Sugar Added Creamsicles
- **Sugar-free fruit-flavored ice pops**
  Sugar Free Popsicles, Crystal Light

Other Dessert Items in the Freezer

- **Mini fillo shells**
  Athens
- **Cool Whip Free**
- **Vitalicious VitaTops**

Cone Zone

- **Cake cones**
- **Sugar cones**

SAUCES, SALAD DRESSINGS, AND SHELF-STABLE CONDIMENTS

Salad Dressings

- **Light, low-fat, and fat-free salad dressings**
  Newman's Own Lighten Up! Low Fat Sesame Ginger Dressing (and other varieties in the Lighten Up! line), Wish-Bone Light, Kraft Free, Kraft Light, low-calorie options from Litehouse, Hidden Valley Fat Free, Girard's Fat Free
- **Spray dressings**
  Wish-Bone Salad Spritzers, Ken's Lite Accents

Vinegars

- **Balsamic (look for flavored varieties, too!)**
- **Seasoned rice vinegar**
- **Apple cider vinegar**
- **Red wine vinegar**

Classic Condiments

- **BBQ sauce (with 45 calories per serving)**
  Chris' & Pitt's, Stubb's
- **Fat-free mayonnaise**
- **Hellmann's/Best Foods Dijonnaise**
- **Mustard (honey, Dijon, spicy brown, yellow)**
- **Vivi's Original Sauce Carnival Mustards (request 'em!)**
- **Ketchup**
  Heinz (No Salt Added, Reduced Sugar, Organic Heinz, Simply Heinz)
- **Hot pepper sauce**
  Frank's RedHot Original Cayenne Pepper Sauce, Tabasco

Other Essentials

- **Reduced-fat peanut butter**
  Skippy Reduced Fat Creamy and Reduced Fat Super Chunk, Justin's Nut Butters (portion-controlled packs)
- **Better'n Peanut Butter/Peanut Wonder**
- **Sugar-free and low-sugar fruit preserves and jam**
  Smucker's Sugar Free and Low Sugar Preserves and Jams, Polaner Sugar Free Preserves with Fiber
- **Thick marinades (30 calories or fewer per tablespoon)**
  Lawry's, Newman's Own, Mrs. Dash
- **Fat-free chicken, beef, and vegetable gravy**

Tomato-Based Sauces and Salsa

- **Low-fat marinara, pasta, and pizza sauce**
  Classico, Dei Fratelli
- **Salsa**
  La Victoria, Pace

Asian Sauces

- **Reduced-sodium/lite soy sauce**
- **Sweet Asian chili sauce**

Mexican Sauces

- **Taco sauce**
- **Enchilada sauce**

Sweet Sauces

- **Sugar-free pancake syrup**
  Cary's Sugar Free, Mrs. Butterworth's Sugar Free, Log Cabin Sugar Free
- **Jet-Puffed Marshmallow Creme**
- **Light and fat-free caramel dip**
  Marzetti Light and Fat Free Caramel Dip, Litehouse Low Fat and Original
- **Light and sugar-free chocolate syrup**
  Hershey's Lite and Sugar Free

BEVERAGES

Water

- **Flavored water**
  Aquafina FlavorSplash, SoBe Lifewater, Vitaminwater Zero, Activate Drinks, Minute Maid Fruit Falls, Just 10 Pouches
- **Coconut water**
  Zico, O.N.E., Vita Coco
- **Spring water**

Juice and Fruit Drinks

- **Light juice beverages**
  Trop50, V8 V-Fusion Light, Ocean Spray Light
- **Low-calorie juice drinks**
  Ocean Spray Diet, Diet V8 Splash (especially Tropical Blend!)
- **Sugar-free powdered drink mixes**
  Crystal Light, Wyler's Light, Lipton Iced Tea To Go, AriZona Sugar Free, True Lemonade, Crystal Light Pure

Soda and Iced Tea

- **Diet soda and club soda**
  Coke Zero, Coke Cherry Zero, Sprite Zero, A&W Diet Root Beer, Dr. Brown's Diet, Blue Sky Free
- **Diet iced tea**
  Diet Snapple (Trop-A-Rocka rocks!), Diet AriZona
- **Unsweetened iced tea**
  Tejava and Gold Peak Tea

Coffee, Cocoa, and Tea

- **Ready-to-brew coffee**
  Millstone, Dunkin' Donuts, K-Cups
- **Instant coffee granules**
  Folgers, Nescafé Taster's Choice
- **Starbucks VIA Ready Brew**
- **Hot cocoa packets with 20 to 25 calories each**
  Swiss Miss Diet, Nestlé Fat Free
- **Tea bags**
  Celestial Seasonings, Tazo, Stash
- **Unsweetened instant iced tea mix**

BAKING PRODUCTS, PANTRY STAPLES, SPICES, AND MORE

Baking Products and Pantry Staples

- Whole-wheat flour
- Cornmeal
- Pancake mix
  Aunt Jemima Whole Wheat Blend Pancake & Waffle Mix, Hungry Jack Complete Extra Light & Fluffy, Fiber One Complete Pancake Mix, Bisquick Heart Smart Pancake and Baking Mix
- Cornstarch
- Baking powder
- Mini semi-sweet chocolate chips
- Peanut butter chips
- Mini marshmallows
- Jet-Puffed Marshmallow Creme
- Shredded sweetened coconut
- Chocolate and rainbow sprinkles
- Unsweetened cocoa powder
- Moist-style cake mixes
  Pillsbury Reduced Sugar Cake Mixes
- Brownie Mix
  No Pudge! Fat Free Fudge Brownie Mix
- Low-fat graham crackers and chocolate graham crackers
- Sugar-free fat-free instant pudding mix
  Jell-O Sugar Free Fat Free Instant
- Nonstick cooking spray
  Pam Original, Pam Professional High Heat, Pam Olive Oil, Pam Butter Flavor
- Olive oil (use sparingly!)
- Fat-free condensed milk

Rice, Pasta, and More

- **Brown rice**
  Birds Eye (freezer aisle)
- **Instant potato flakes**
  Betty Crocker 80 Calories Per Serving Pouch Potatoes
- **High-fiber and whole-wheat-blend pasta**
  Ronzoni Healthy Harvest and Smart Taste, Barilla Plus and Whole Grain
- **House Foods Tofu Shirataki Noodle Substitute**
  (in the refrigerated tofu section)
- **Wonton wrappers**
- **Egg roll wrappers**

Sweeteners, Etc.

- **No-calorie sweetener packets**
  Splenda, Truvia, Pure Via, Stevia Extract In The Raw, Sun Crystals
- **Splenda No Calorie Sweetener, granulated (comes loose in the box)**
- **Powdered sugar**
- **Granulated white sugar**
- **Brown sugar**
- **Sugar-free calorie-free flavored syrups**
  Torani Sugar Free Syrups
- **Sugar-free and fat-free flavored powdered creamer**
  Coffee-mate Sugar Free and Fat Free French Vanilla
- **Fat-free plain powdered creamer**
  Coffee-mate Fat Free The Original

Spices, Extracts, and Seasonings

- **Vanilla extract**
- **Coconut extract**
- **Cinnamon**
- **Garlic powder**
- **Onion powder**
- **Italian seasoning**
- **Dried minced onion**
- **Pumpkin pie spice**
- **Dry taco, fajita, and chili seasoning mix**
- **Dry onion soup/dip mix**
- **Dry ranch dressing/dip mix**
- **Jarred chopped garlic**

Well, there you have it.
The Official Hungry Girl Supermarket Guide.
Hope it makes your food shopping
experiences easier and more fun. If you
have any comments or suggestions,
email 'em to suggest@hungry-girl.com.
See ya in the aisles . . .

INDEX

hot dogs, 38
lean burger patties, 33
lean ground, 32
Meat 'n Seafood by the Numbers, 43
patties, sausage, and pepperoni, 33
slices, 37
turnips, 58, 64, 77

U
Unsweetened Vanilla Almond Breeze,
18, 203

V
Vanilla Almond Breeze, 18, 203
vanilla extract, 196
vanilla soymilk, 18, 203, 209
vegetables. *See* **canned vegetables;
fresh vegetables; frozen vegetables**
vegetarian. *See* **meatless**
veggie burgers, 47, 51, 212
Veggies to Bake Into Fries!, 58
vinegars, 150–51, 199
Vitalicious VitaTops, 127, 143, 199
Vitaminwater Zero, 168, 171, 224
Vivi's Original Sauce Classic Carnival
Mustard, 199

W
waffles, 126
water, 168–69
watermelon, 73, 77
Weight Watchers, 208, 218, 219,
220, 221
Which One When?
hamburger-style patties vs.
veggie-burger patties, 47
jarred marinara, pasta, or pizza
sauce vs. canned crushed
tomatoes, 159
Reddi-wip vs. Cool Whip, 15
whipped topping, 15, 138, 142, 183
whole grains
Food Faker Alert!, 116
Whole Grain 101, 187
whole-wheat flour, 178, 225
Wish-Bone, 148, 149, 222

wonton wrappers, 190

Y
yams, 58, 62
yellow squash, 64, 77
yogurt, 12–13, 208
Apple BFFs!, 71
frozen, 136, 138

Z
zucchini, 60, 64, 77